BY THE EDITORS OF CONSUMER GUIDE®
WITH PHILLIP J. KAPLAN

THE BEST, WORST & MOST UNUSUAL:
HOLLYWOOD MUSICALS

BEEKMAN HOUSE
New York

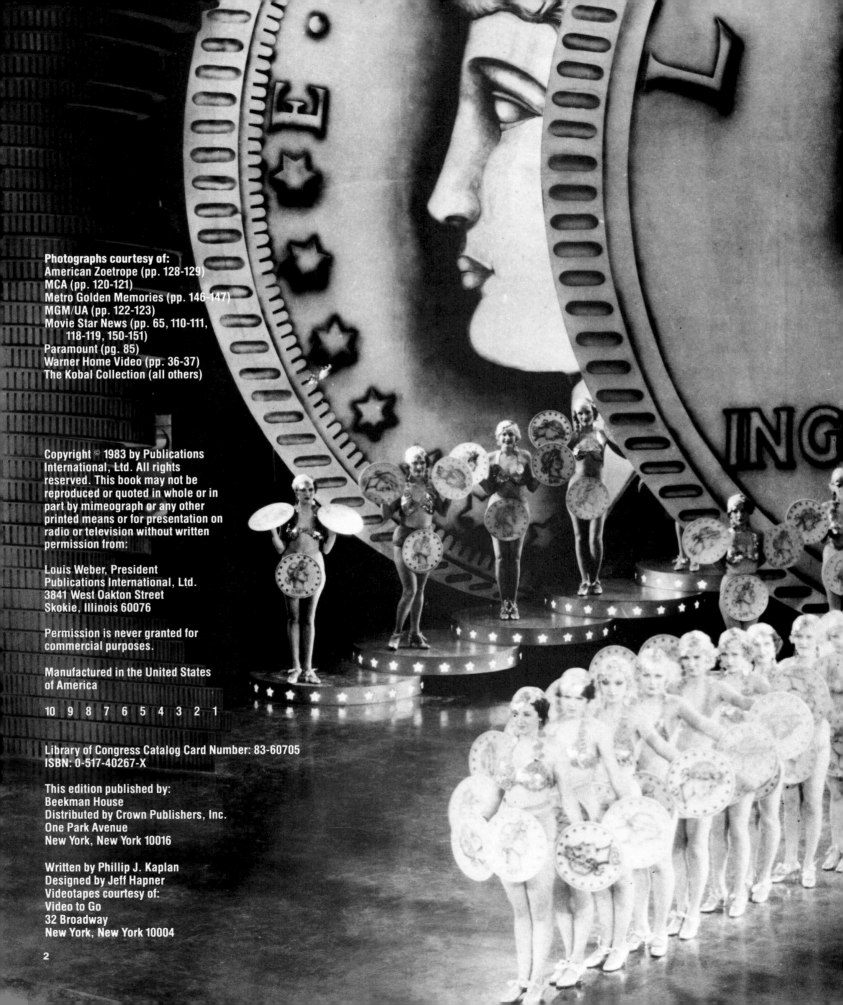

Photographs courtesy of:
American Zoetrope (pp. 128-129)
MCA (pp. 120-121)
Metro Golden Memories (pp. 146-147)
MGM/UA (pp. 122-123)
Movie Star News (pp. 65, 110-111, 118-119, 150-151)
Paramount (pg. 85)
Warner Home Video (pp. 36-37)
The Kobal Collection (all others)

Louis Weber, President
Publications International, Ltd.
3841 West Oakton Street
Skokie, Illinois 60076

10 9 8 7 6 5 4 3 2 1

Library of Congress Catalog Card Number: 83-60705
ISBN: 0-517-40267-X

This edition published by:
Beekman House
Distributed by Crown Publishers, Inc.
One Park Avenue
New York, New York 10016

Written by Phillip J. Kaplan
Designed by Jeff Hapner
Videotapes courtesy of:
Video to Go
32 Broadway
New York, New York 10004

2

Busby Berkeley imagines that "We're In the Money" with a Depression fantasy that is both visually inventive and wishfulfilling. This sequence occurs in Gold Diggers of 1933.

Title Page: **The Ziegfield Follies**

Final Page: **Gentlemen Prefer Blondes**

3

CONTENTS

Fred Astaire and Judy Garland are just "A Couple of Swells." This rendition of a vaudeville act is from Easter Parade (1948).

FOREWORD

This is a book about watching movies. That is, this is a book about connections—about watching movie after movie after movie. This is more than a rating guide (although a rating guide appears at the back), or a reference book (although it should answer most of your questions about individual films). This is first and foremost a movie book—a book about what it means to watch movies.

Although primarily intended for those with access to a videotape or disc player, THE BEST, WORST & MOST UN-USUAL: HOLLYWOOD MUSI-CALS is a book for any fan of the musical genre.

The magic about videotapes and discs is that, suddenly, *you* own the theatre. You decide which movie plays on your marquee. You can plan out a strategy for watching musicals that will provide maximum enjoyment of the films' interconnections. For instance, you might want to watch all of Busby Berkeley's movies together, or see all the Fred Astaire-Ginger Rogers movies

in chronological order. The well-chosen double-feature can add a new dimension to each film. THE BEST, WORST & MOST UNUSUAL: HOLLY-WOOD MUSICALS is written to help you make these choices. The interesting connections, homages, remakes, star vehicles and directorial coups are all pointed out in addition to individual reviews.

An American in Paris *(1951).*

6

Unfortunately, there are still many great musicals that are unavailable on tape or disc. However, if they're in this book, they will probably be released eventually.

There are several critical differences between watching movies on tape and watching them in a theatre. The big difference is, of course, the size. These

films were made to be shown larger-than-life. The reduction in size often results in a substantial reduction in impact. A second difference concerns a duplication process called scanning. The home TV screen is never wide enough to show the entire image area of a movie screen. These problems are compounded if the film was

shot in CinemaScope, or some other "super-wide" format. When these films are transferred to video, the screen may be scanned on where the action is. This means that you may miss something that is critical to the enjoyment of this film.

Nonetheless, we continue to sing the praises of videotape and disc players. These relatively inexpensive machines have placed the entire history of film potentially at your fingertips. And for musicals, the sound provided on laser disc is often better than that in a movie theatre. Surprisingly, more films watched on video, the more often people go to movie theatres. Videotape simply starts a process that becomes more and more addictive. There is no better way to start or fuel that addiction than with this book. Start anywhere and follow your leads.

We have provided a strong critical guidance. We may hate the films you love or love the films you hate. But, then, that's what movie-watching is all about.

"The Best" films comprise most of this book. The rest of the space is devoted to the curiosities: "The Worst" and the "Most Unusual." The worst are the real trash, the ones

you've got to see. The unusual are, at times, the most interesting. Combined, the Best, Worst, and Most Unusual truly recreate the fun of movie going, where the good are made especially good in comparison with the strange and the trash.

This book on musicals is one in a series of film genre books. Look for even more titles in the future. We are determined to bring you the best written, most attractive books on film.

LET'S FACE THE MUSIC AND DANCE

hen talking about the movie
usical it is easy to slip into
e past tense. The genre looks
 but gone now. Although
ere are a few musicals put
t each year they seem like
itches in a nearly lifeless
dy. Even when the good
usicals appear, their success
minds us of the heyday of
e Hollywood musical when
zens of great musicals were
eased every year.

one time, musicals were the
ost popular type of film. In
27 *The Jazz Singer* ushered
 the sound movie era as well
 the musical. The novelty of
e musical revue caused audi-

ences to flock to the films that
followed, most of which were
quite bad. To be fair, the
filmmakers of 1928 and 1929
had so many technical sound-
related problems to surmount
that the quality of their film
could easily be neglected. For
example, in *Broadway Melody*
the girls wore costumes of
spangled beads, that is, until
their clinking sound showed
up on the soundtrack. In *The
Cocoanuts*, every time someone carried a piece of paper it
would crackle like a thunder-
storm. Solution: douse each
page in water. Small wonder
that early musicals often
seem crude.

However, the technical challenges seemed to pique the imaginations of the most talented
people. The witty and stylish
Ernst Lubitsch, director of
many popular light romantic
comedies, was the first to rise
above the limitations of sound
filmmaking and explore the im-
mense possibilities of staging
musical numbers for film. His
1929 musical, *The Love Parade*, showcased the love-duets

more intimately and with more
subtle detailing than theatrical
performances could allow. He
was the first to realize that
films could be more romantic
than plays because the camera
could go in close with the
lovers.

The greatest challenge of sound filmmaking—camera mobility—was sufficiently solved by the early 1930s for production numbers to move freely about. Another Lubitsch operetta, *Monte Carlo*, coordinates a moving train and a rhythmic tune to create an exciting context for its musical number.

Hollywood always kept its sights trained on Broadway for new material, even though it chronically did better with original musicals. Cole Porter's hit show, "Anything Goes," seemed so promising that it was attempted cinematically twice, 1934 and 1956 (shown here). Even with fabulous songs, they couldn't capture its spirit.

Ironically though, as musicals got better and better, the public began to lose interest. By early 1933, musicals looked like a passing fad. But it only takes one hit to start a new trend, and in 1933 there were two: *42nd Street* and *Flying Down to Rio*. *42nd Street* introduced the choreography of Busby Berkeley and *Flying Down to Rio* introduced the dancing of Fred Astaire and Ginger Rogers.

Choreographer Busby Berkeley was the man most responsible for lifting the musical out of its primitive era. The genius of Berkeley was that he realized that the camera was the most important element in a screen dance. For example, a line of girls standing still is hardly interesting, but pan a camera past each of their faces and a dance is created by the movement of the camera. Berkeley utilized his camera in a variety of ways. His famous overhead shots often involved a group of dancers on a revolving stage. When shot from above, the dancers formed a continually changing geometric pattern. Another Berkeley trademark was the bizarre chorus line. Be it hundreds of girls playing neon violins, or hundreds of girls diving into the water, the effect was always incredible. But Berkeley did not always need a huge chorus to create a stunning effect. Sometimes he could wow the audience simply by camera movement. He delighted in zooming in on performers, only to zoom out again with his singers suddenly in a completely new set. Using the camera's ability to isolate, Berkeley was able to film scene changes and transitions that could never have happened on a Broadway stage.

At the opposite end of Berkeley's camera tricks were the flawless and uninterrupted performances of Fred Astaire. Before Fred Astaire, the dance musical was nonexistent. Mostly, people just sang. Any attempt at choreography was usually lost amid the spectacle of a huge production number. Busby Berkeley didn't even use dancing in his films; at

best his chorus would walk in a line while the camera whizzed by. Fred Astaire's impact on the musical cannot be over-estimated because he was the first performer to take charge of his physical presence in the film frame. His dancing transported musicals to new heights in both expertise and personal involvement.

One can see the changes that Astaire wrought even in his first film, *Flying Down to Rio*. Though they only had bit parts (sixth on the star billing), he and Ginger Rogers still managed to steal the film with The Carioca, a dance which became a nationwide craze because of them. The warmth and expressiveness of his great partner, Ginger, made their duets into personal and romantic statements. Audiences were more interested in their interactions than Greta Garbo's love speeches. Because of its intimate nature, Astaire realized that photography could make or break a dance. Previously, dance numbers were filmed haphazardly, but Fred Astaire insisted that his entire body be visible throughout. Astaire danced with his entire body; the position of his hands was as important as that of his feet. He also kept editing to a minimum, so that the rhythms of his movements would remain continuous.

The films that Fred Astaire and Ginger Rogers made together will remain high points of the musical genre forever. Not only were they witty, sophisticated, and stylish, but their emphasis on dance created a more total entertainment experience. The films also benefited from some the finest tunes by the best songwriters of their day.

The 1930s was a time of diverse entertainers. While Fred and Ginger provided sophisticated entertainment, another singer supplied a more innocent joy. Shirley Temple was rewarded for her innocence by becoming the biggest star in the world. She was the ultimate performer: she could sing, dance, and act.

In the late 60s and early 70s, the musical suffered from an overdose of money. In a manic effort to create a hit out of his Broadway success, director Bob Fosse blew Sweet Charity *(1969) all out of proportion. A modest play, it became a gaudy, if energetic, dinosaur of a movie.*

Teenage dance socials turn out a little differently when the kids are as tough as those in West Side Story.

She wasn't just a great child actress, she was great, *period*. Because it was recognized that she wouldn't be an adorable little girl forever, her studio churned out dozens of films in her prepubescence.

By the end of the 1930s, however, it looked like the musical was losing steam again. Busby Berkeley left his home studio of Warner Brothers. Fred Astaire and Ginger Rogers split up as dance partners. And, alas, Shirley Temple grew up. But just at this time, Metro-Goldwyn-Mayer came to the rescue. Their studio formula for making musicals suddenly came together splendorously in 1939 with *The Wizard of Oz*. Over the next twenty years MGM would dominate the field of musicals, consistently making the best, the most innovative and most popular films. Their record of quality is unequalled.

One man must take credit for MGM's fabulous track record: Arthur Freed. Freed was the producer of the musicals that stand out as MGM's masterpieces. He began his career on *The Wizard of Oz*, where his fight to keep in the song, "Somewhere Over the Rainbow," proved his intelligence and insight. A hit songwriter himself, Freed knew the value of creative freedom. His formula for success was simple: Find the best people and give them rein to create. He brought Gene Kelly to Hollywood and allowed him to choreograph and direct. Kelly's energetic talent fused the polarities of Astaire and Berkeley; he made the camera his dance partner. Without a producer like Freed who was willing to experiment, no dancer could have gained as much access to filmmaking as Kelly did. Freed also brought Vincente Minnelli to films.

Freed's films contain such a vital integration of elements because all his people worked so closely as a team. Minnelli's experience as a set designer enabled him to make use of his sets more fully. Kelly's experience as an actor, dancer, and choreographer made him an ideal director because he could anticipate problems. Freed himself shared artistic control and input. When Donald O'Connor

needed a song in *Singin' in the Rain,* Freed wrote "Make 'Em Laugh" in 15 minutes. Among Freed's list of major achievements are: *The Wizard of Oz, Meet Me in St. Louis, The Pirate, An American in Paris, Singin' in the Rain, The Band Wagon, Brigadoon* and *Gigi.*

Vincente Minnelli is arguably the best MGM director, and cer-tainly the most distinctive. All his films contain a strong fusion between story and song and a striking use of color. His masterpiece is *Meet Me in St. Louis,* in which he creates an entire world in song and color. He had an ambitious streak and constantly strove to expand the boundaries of the musical. He introduced ballet dance movement to musicals in *Yolanda and the Thief* and *The Pirate.* He managed to elicit serious statements out of the musical in *An American in Paris* and *The Band Wagon.* He created dazzling fantasy sequences in *The Ziegfield Follies* and *Brigadoon.* Minnelli strove for perfection in a genre that demanded excellence to begin with, and often achieved it.

13

In the 1950s the musical shifted gears again. Up until then most movie musicals were written for the screen. This meant that an idea would be conceived with motion pictures in mind and could be made cinematic from the outset. It also meant that each film would have songs especially commissioned, making the successful ones all the more impressive. It is one thing to assemble songs which are already famous and make a good movie, as in the case of the Irving Berlin songs in *Easter Parade*, but it is quite another thing for Mr. Berlin to write the score for *Top Hat* and then have every one of those songs become a classic. Virtually all of America's great songwriters wrote for Hollywood at one point. These included Cole Porter, George Gershwin, Jerome Kern, Harold Arlen, Rodgers and Hart, Harry Warren and, of course, Irving Berlin.

In the late 1940s and early 1950s movie attendance declined. Studios had to cut back productions. Costs were mounting and every film *had* to succeed. Instead of gambling on original material, Hollywood frantically tried to adapt proven Broadway musicals for the screen. This was not as easy as it sounds. Broadway musicals are written for the stage, not for the camera. The average Broadway musical is two-and-a-half hours long—the average film 90 minutes. Studios had the choice of either cutting the material, faithfully keeping everything from the play, or judiciously rewriting and reworking things. They tried all three approaches. Although the quality of these adaptations was usually not as high as most original Hollywood musicals, they proved crowd pleasers. As a result, the bulk of musicals from the 1960s and 1970s were Broadway adaptations, including *The Sound of Music, The Pajama Game, The King and I*, and *Cabaret*.

The success of Broadway based movies proved misleading. For instance, *The Sound of Music* was one of the highest grossing films ever. Unfortunately, Hollywood learned all the wrong things from that film, concluding that the more money one spends on a film the better it would be. Finally, in the 1970s, there came a string of multi-million dollar musical dinosaurs that bombed. Among them were *Lost Horizon, At Long Last Love*, and *Mame*—inept and over-budgeted disasters that delivered a killing blow to the musical.

It was the studios' own fault. What these films lacked was a sense of proportion and interaction. A fabulous set is useless without dynamic personalities within it. Good singers need good songs. Performances need camerawork that supports them. The studios could no longer provide this, because when they cut back and stopped doing original creative work, the whole studio system changed.

The whole concept of studios is a little difficult to grasp today. Now, the only thing that identifies a studio is its logo, but in the 1930s and 1940s each studio had its own distinctive style. Warner's films were fast-paced, realistic and often uncompromising (i.e., *Public Enemy, Casablanca, 42nd Street*). At the opposite extreme there was MGM, whose films were lavish, polished and tended toward fantasy, (*Mutiny on the Bounty, Grand Hotel, Gone With the Wind*). As long as there were eight studios there would be at least eight styles of musicals. With the collapse of the studios this diversity ended.

Even more important, the studio system also assured that films would be technically competent. When studios were big and turning out 40 pictures a year, they could afford a department whose sole responsibility was designing costumes. They could also keep a full-sized orchestra busily at work. At any moment, the studio had on call a group of trained specialists in whatever technical field was needed. No genre needed this craftsmanship more than the musical. Everything had to be perfect in order for it to work.

The musical has done rather well at using modern dance in choreography. Some of Twyla Tharp's work in Hair.

The dancing must be photographed seamlessly, the sets must not be distracting, the singing must be audible—the slightest hitch and the whole artifice collapses. The musical is, after all, a fantasy genre trying to pass itself off as something normal. Most musicals operate as dreams within the real world. We know that in real life people don't sing in restaurants or dance in the streets during thunderstorms, yet when all of the elements work together it is easy to accept these stylizations.

However, what happens quite often in many of the inept contemporary musicals is that the elements don't work together. For instance, in *Annie*, when the cute orphan kids start to do their incredibly clumsy dance, something looks wrong because this number is poorly choreographed and filmed. The audience has to struggle to figure out just what the kids are doing, and then they start to wonder why. The stylization does not work because the awkward filming has burst the bubble. Musicals cannot be sloppy.

Quite apart from the decline of the craft of musicals is the fact that moviemakers lost touch with musical styles. In the 1930s and 1940s, musicals were right on top of the current trends. If Benny Goodman was hot, he would soon find himself on a movie set. If girls were fainting over Frank Sinatra at his concerts, the movie moguls were smart enough to let him sing in their musicals and let the girls faint at his films. In the 1950s the first noticeable split arose between movie musicals and popular music. Hollywood was confused about rock 'n' roll. The craftsmen who were so adept at arranging, adapting, staging, recording, and filming Cole Porter tunes didn't know what to do with "Blue Suede Shoes." They brought in Elvis Presley, the biggest rock 'n' roll star, and then buried him in a series of witless musicals that had nothing to do with the rock 'n' roll audience. His persona was watered down, but his fans went to see him anyway. This unfortunate paradox

kept the producers from trying more innovative approaches.

In the 1960s and 1970s, rock 'n' roll *became* "American Popular Music", and there was no musical format to contain it. In addition, the average age of movie audiences dropped into the teenage bracket. This meant that for a musical to be popular, it had to be a rock musical. Musicals could not make the transition. The problem was that up until this point the musical had been built around telling a very simple story in complex songs and dances. Now, the audience wanted more sophisticated stories told through simpler, more emotional songs. Rock 'n' roll does not fit into the slower context, but does not help to progress a story on its own, either. The problem can be seen in films such as *The Wiz*, in which the rock songs work well as rock songs, but actually slow down the action and become redundant. The world is still waiting for a good story musical utilizing rock music.

The most interesting musicals being made today do not try to tell a story *through* the music, but *about* the music. The rise of realistic musical dramas about performers offers the most satisfying present day version of the musical. Films like *The Rose* and *Coal Miner's Daughter* give us credible dramas about musical personalities and present their music as real events within the film.

The musical isn't dead, it's simply waiting for that new trend that will launch it in another direction. With fewer movies being produced every year, the chances of that unknown musical rising up out of the chorus and becoming the star of the show become slimmer, but it will happen. Even as fans of the musical look fondly back at the glory days of the past, they keep their eyes peeled for that new Ernst Lubitsch, that new Busby Berkeley or Vincente Minnelli, the Gene Kelly or Fred Astaire of the 1980s. Reality dictates that the chances are slim, but after all, it happens in musicals all the time.

THE BEST OF BACKSTAGE MUSICALS

42ND STREET (1933)
THE BAND WAGON (1953)
CABARET (1972)
BROADWAY MELODY (1929)
FOOTLIGHT PARADE (1933)
GOLD DIGGERS OF 1933 (1933)
BABES IN ARMS (1939)
HOLIDAY INN (1942)
BLUE SKIES (1946)
SUMMER STOCK (1950)
SINGIN' IN THE RAIN (1952)

"When a Broadway baby says goodnight,
It's early in the morning."

"Lullaby of Broadway"
Al Dubin and Harry Warren

Jakie Rabinowitz (Al Jolson) romances his showgirl sweetheart
(May McAvoy) between performances in The Jazz Singer.

17

42ND STREET (1933) is the archetypal backstage musical: the star of a show breaks her leg on the opening night, and an unknown girl from the chorus line rises up to save the show and become a star. *42nd Street* created many of the axioms and techniques that have become clichés through overuse in other films. Movie dialogue lines like "You're going out there a youngster, but you've *got* to come back a star!" have become standard expressions. *42nd Street* rises well above the morass of familiar situations because of its pure spark of originality; the film is as exuberant and fresh as the young hopefuls in the chorus line.

"*Naughty, bawdy, gaudy, sporty* 42nd Street."

The structure of *42nd Street* sets the standard for most backstage musicals, an enduring form. The structure of a backstage musical allows for both character development (in rehearsal) and lavish spectacle (in the finished play). In the beginning, someone decides to create a show. Then some great need for the show to succeed emerges; in *42nd Street*, director Julian Marsh (Warner Baxter) is broke and needs money to retire because his health is failing. The difficult process of casting and rehearsal introduces the characters and shows how hard they work.

42nd Street is meant to be a film of contrasts. The leads are sweet and innocent, but everyone around them seems a bit lecherous. The show people are thick-skinned and cynical, yet they follow their dreams of stardom at any cost. The star of the show is torn between her career and her love life. The final irony comes in the last moments as the audience streams out of the hit show. The director, who has slaved away to the point of suicide, has done his job so well that the public thinks he has coasted along on a great show and cast. It is the lot of show biz technicians for their most successful efforts to become invisible. The Broadway life comes alive in *42nd Street* because it isn't glossed over. The pain, frustration, and desperation surface. The director sums it all up in one of his stirring speeches: "You're going to work and sweat and work some more . . . you're going to dance until your feet fall off, and you're not able to stand up any longer. But five weeks from now, we're going to have a show."

Some of the characters in *42nd Street* are unforgettable, like the starry-eyed and naive Diane Sawyer (Ruby Keeler) and the everything-but-naive Anytime Annie (Ginger Rogers), who "only said 'No' once, and even then she didn't hear the question." Once the characters have been introduced, something traumatic typically happens; in *42nd Street*, it's that broken leg. Crisis is averted just in time for the film to explode into sumptuous feasts of song and dance. The eye-popping spectacles that *42nd Street* yields to at its end not only set the form for other musicals to follow, but they also hold their own against all the production numbers that came later.

The final third of *42nd Street* is almost completely filled with the big production numbers from Marsh's play, "Pretty Lady." Busby Berkeley's unique ideas about cinema choreography burst across the screen like fireworks. His keen eye for perspective and editing turns the limbs of chorus girls into a kaleidoscope and expands a small Broadway stage into an entire city block. Trying to figure out the plot of "Pretty Lady" from its set pieces is fun. "Shuffle Off to Buffalo" takes place between newly-weds on a train to Niagara Falls, they start out singing off the caboose, which splits in half to reveal the compartments within. "Young and Healthy" features Berkeley's famous human kaleidoscope and a somewhat lascivious invitation by Dick Powell. "Pretty Lady" ends with "42nd Street," a celebration of that raucous and exciting district. This number is a mini-musical in itself, in which the action begins on a small theatre stage but expands onto a full city block.

42nd Street works because it looks, sounds, and feels authentic. The wonderfully cynical script wouldn't work in a pretty, make-believe world. When the show must have a trial run in Philadelphia, the star complains, "But I don't want to go to Philadelphia." The director's response, "Who does?" makes perfect sense. *42nd Street* conveys not only the excitement and raw energy that goes into making a show, but also the heartache and sense of futility that comes from working on Broadway.

Girls turn into dancing skylines in an early Busby Berkeley perspective trick.

Director Julian Marsh (Warner Baxter) selects his chorus girls from an open casting call in 42nd Street.

a backstage musical that doubles as a declaration of principles for the MGM musical. It is a great story musical, expertly combining plot, characters, and songs into a unified whole. It is lush and lyrical, brash and bright, arty and artistic, self-parodying and heartfelt, and above all, entertaining. The film amazingly balances all its levels and relates them to the theme of entertainment. "That's Entertainment," one of the best numbers in the film, went on to become the theme song of MGM.

The Band Wagon is a classic case of art imitating life. Fred Astaire appeared in *The Band Wagon* when it was on Broadway, and 20 years later that sense of history and continuity shaped the filmscript by Betty Comden and Adolph Green. The film version is about Fred Astaire's movie legend. Astaire plays Tony Hunter, a down-on-his-luck Hollywood song-and-dance man once at the top of his profession. In New York, Lester and Lily Marton (Oscar Levant and Nanette Fabray) have written a new musical for him. They have engaged Jeffrey Cordova (Jack Buchanan) —a wunderkind who stages, choreographs, acts, and even translates—to direct and Gabrielle Gerard (Cyd Charisse), a ballet dancer, to co-star. Hunter is wary. He feels he can't compete with Gerard, and doesn't think Cordova can direct a musical.

Cordova convinces everyone that he knows what he's doing, and the whole process of producing a play begins. During the backer's audition, Cordova acts out the show, which now sounds suspiciously like *Faust*. He designs cumbersome and arty scenery, rewrites the script, helps choreograph the dances and finally opens the show in New Haven. An enthusiastic theatre crowd is excited at the prospect of seeing a new musical, but after the opening a crowd of shaken people exits as if they've just witnessed an autopsy. Tony Hunter, the song-and-dance man, takes over direction of

the show. He puts the fun songs back in and creates a hit. It has that secret of theatrical success: entertainment.

While Fred Astaire is Tony Hunter's real-life counterpart, Jeffrey Cordova is director Vincente Minnelli taken to extremes. Minnelli was interested in broadening the scope of movie musicals in such films as *Yolanda and the Thief, The Ziegfield Follies* and *An American in Paris*. Cordova wants to break down musical barriers and says things like "In my mind there is no difference between the magic rhythms of Bill Shakespeare's immortal verse and the magic rhythms of Bill Robinson's immortal feet." The film mocks this attitude by having Cordova mangle the classics as thoroughly as he mangles musicals. Cordova believes in "Art" with a capital A, and doesn't know how to make something serious that is also fun.

The Martons are the Comden and Green surrogates in the film. They are writers and also performers, as were Comden and Green in their early Broadway days. Since Comden and Green wrote the script, the writers are treated sympathetically. After they explain their concept for a light and intimate show, Cordova explains his version of it as a Faustian parable ending with "His sellout must end in eternal damnation!" Lester Marton, resigned to his fate, sighs "That'll leave 'em laughing."

The songs by Arthur Schwartz and Howard Dietz are superb. A depressed and lonely Tony Hunter walks through a railroad station singing that he will go through life "By Myself," and in "A Shine on Your Shoes," he romps through a penny arcade, dancing his way past mirrors and fortune-telling machines. "That's Entertainment," the film's fun anthem, has Buchanan, Levant, Fabray, and Astaire clowning around, doing vaudeville parodies, and dancing while they sing that entertainment is "some great Shakespearean scene, where a ghost and a prince meet, and everyone ends in mincemeat." Charisse and Astaire stroll together in a set of Central Park. As the music swells they gradually segue into "Dancing in the Dark"—a serious dance with ballet overtones. The beautiful dreamlike setting creates a romantic atmosphere. "Triplets" is the funniest song in the show. Fabray, Astaire, and Buchanan play three little babies dressed in white bonnets who do everything alike and wish they had a "widdle gun . . . to shoot the other two and be only one."

The climactic finale is a half-witted satire of Mickey Spillane novels called "The Girl Hunt Ballet." Choreographed by Michael Kidd, it is one of those spectacular MGM entire-story-in-one-number pieces. Unlike its compatriot pieces in *Singin' in the Rain* and *An American in Paris*, "The Girl Hunt Ballet" is poorly conceived. Its arty pretensions seem derived from the Jeffrey Cordova side of Vincente Minnelli.

The Band Wagon succeeds because, though obviously personal, it is never self indulgent. It is a meditation on fame, the functions of directors, and the lot of theatrical people, but it stays fun. And that's truly entertainment.

In the "The Girl Hunt Ballet," Fred Astaire is a hard-boiled detective on the trail of "a rag, a bone, and a hunk of hair." His sleuthing lands the beautiful, "bad, dangerous" Cyd Charisse in his arms.

The rise of Nazism, and the indifference of ordinary people toward it, is reflected in the powerful musical **CABARET** (1972). By concentrating on the inhabitants of a decadent nightclub, the film shows the manner in which many people ignore turbulent social events by desperately searching for fun. *Cabaret* shows both the fun and the pain, with unwavering honesty. Using the backstage musical for serious purposes, *Cabaret* performs a daring feat—it creates a frighteningly real world and uses music to convey the horror.

In the decadent society of pre-World War II Germany, young British writer Brian (Michael York) meets and falls in love with Sally Bowles (Liza Minnelli), a cabaret singer and prostitute. Sally is an extraordinary character who needs constant thrills to stay alive. Songs clearly define her character at every stage of the film. In "Mein Herr" she explains why she's breaking off an affair: "You'll never turn the vinegar to jam, Mein Herr," and then starts another ill-fated affair with Brian. But "Cabaret" is the song which gives the clearest understanding of Sally. She has decided to stay in Germany and explains that it's best to have fun while you can: "No use permitting some prophet of doom to wipe every smile away."

The stage version's subplot about an old Jewish fruit store owner and his affair with a German landlady was dropped from the movie. This changed the tone of the story drastically. The show was a humorous one with serious undertones, but the film is a serious one with only occasional humorous notes. The film is a more literal adaptation of *I Am a Camera*, the book by Christopher Isherwood on which *Cabaret* is based. At the opening the Master of Ceremonies (Joel Grey), a ghostly looking man with pale skin, rouged lips, and a satanic smile, welcomes all with "Willkommen." The seediness and decadence of Germany is immediately established with shots of an audience resembling George Grosz sketches. The smoke-filled Kit Kat Club represents the jaded society beyond its walls.

Musical numbers show the slow rise of Nazism in Germany: a mud wrestling act in the cabaret between two women at the end of which Master of Ceremonies Joel Grey gives himself a Hitler mustache with some of the mud; a beer barrel dance involving actors comically slapping each other is intercut with shots of a Jewish businessman being viciously beaten in a nearby alley; and

The smoky sleaziness of the all-girl (one suspects) band in Cabaret *visually complements the decadent atmosphere of the Kit Kat Club.*

"If You Could See Her," in which the MC talks about his girlfriend whom everyone thinks ugly. She is revealed to be a gorilla, and the number is amusing until the last line which says, "If you could see her through my eyes, she wouldn't look Jewish at all." A truly chilling moment occurs in the only song set outside the cabaret. At an outdoor café a young Nazi starts singing "Tomorrow Belongs to Me," his swastika armband painfully visible. The camera focuses on the people in the crowd as they listen. There is momentary indecision about joining in. Suddenly one boy stands up, and others follow, fervently joining in the song. The scene shows how the Nazis intimidated others to join, and also shows that people wanted to be convinced.

Slickly directed by Bob Fosse, *Cabaret* was justly showered with Oscars when it came out: best director, best actress, and best supporting actor. Geoffrey Unsworth, the director of photography, was responsible for the stunning visual design of the film—a seductive yet threatening gloss which gives even ordinary scenes an ominous aura. Michael York, as the naive lead hero, is appropriately bland. Liza Minnelli is flamboyant and uncontrolled and too good a performer for the sleazy Kit Kat Club. Joel Grey gives the most memorable performance; his presence is felt throughout the movie and there are many reaction shots of him intercut with other scenes. After "Tomorrow Belongs to Me," there is a shot of Grey, whose snide look alone conveys the inevitability of the Nazi's takeover.

Liza Minnelli confides that life is a Cabaret.

BROADWAY MELODY (1929) was the first really good back-stage musical. When sound was first used in the movies, singing and Broadway-style musical revues were very popular. The best way to incorporate these elements into a story was to make the story about the events behind a Broadway show. *Broadway Melody* was the first of these early attempts to be successful in both its story and its songs.

Broadway Melody is a tear-jerking story about two sisters (played by Anita Page and Bessie Love) trying to make it big as "The Harmony Girls of Melody Lane." The harmony of their relationship is strained when one sister loses both a starring role and her boy-friend to the other. Although the basic story is silly and shamelessly sentimental, the dialogue is good and the performances are inspired. Bessie Love as "Hank" is especially impressive. Her scene in front of her dressing-room mirror—in which she tries to control her emotions—is one of the most memorable moments in film. Love's performance won her an Oscar nomination. Love is still acting today; her most recent appearance was in *Ragtime*.

Charles King struts his stuff.

24

The presentation of the music is rather awkward. Songs are either served up in flat production numbers or presented as actual events. Either way, it's disorienting. The most embarrassing moment occurs when Bessie Love is being courted by her leading man, Eddie. Suddenly, the background music swells and Eddie bursts into: "You Were Meant for Me." It is a jarring moment.

Later films would better integrate the reality of their stories with the illusion of the musical numbers. Films like *Broadway Melody* had to make their mistakes first. Although the mistakes are forever frozen on film, *Broadway Melody* is too good to be shelved as a mere museum piece. It is a relic of a transitional stage in the motion picture musical.

Broadway Melody featured the first songs ever conceived and written directly for a film, including the title song and "You Were Meant for Me" by Arthur Freed and Nacio Herb Brown.

FOOTLIGHT PARADE (1933) is unique among the early backstage musicals in that it acknowledged the world of movies. It is still set in the Broadway world of *42nd Street* though, and bears many similarities to that film, most prominently the choreography of Busby Berkeley. James Cagney plays a Broadway producer who finds the funding for his show withdrawn when his financiers fear that the public will flock to the cinema instead. The savvy Cagney effects a compromise: he proposes to put on musical numbers at three separate movie houses as a prologue to the main feature. The wisecracking cast is fun to watch; they are either at each other's throats or madly dashing from theatre to theatre. The behind-the-scenes story eventually gives way to big production numbers.

There is a huge rambling story number, "Honeymoon Hotel," which has house detectives trying to figure out why everyone who registers is named Smith. "By a Waterfall," by Sammy Fain and Irving Kahal, is an amazing geometric number, shot from underneath the glass bottom of a specially built aquarium full of bathing beauties. The finale, "Shanghai Lil," is another bizarre story number extending over much space and time. James Cagney is a sailor who's been looking high and low, "looking for my Shanghai Lil." He searches many stylized Oriental bars and nightclubs. When he finally finds her, it's Ruby Keeler looking about as Oriental as Myron Cohen. Next the scene jumps to marching troops who hold up cards that fill the screen with the image of the NRA eagle; they turn the cards over, and there's Franklin Roosevelt! The quirky ending has Cagney, who has jumped ship to stay with Keeler, pull out a cartoon flipbook. He flips it and shows a cartoon of a ship sailing away. *Footlight Parade* sails through its course just as smoothly and cleverly.

GOLD DIGGERS OF 1933 (1933), a fast-paced, funny film, tracks the attempts of several chorus girls to marry wealthy men. It appropriately starts with "We're in the Money," a Depression fantasy. Girls tap-dance in costumes of silver dollars, with huge coins hung in the background and on the floor. The highlight is when Ginger Rogers races through the pig latin version of the song. To emphasize that no one is in the money, the number ends when the creditors close the show. The rest of the picture is a rollicking collection of plots, tunes, and elaborate dance numbers. "The Shadow Waltz" is definitely removed from reality. The chorines wear puffy white dresses that stick out like giant moth wings. They seem to float as they dance on a long, twisting staircase and play white violins. Then the lights dim and the violins light up, rimmed in neon. Shrouded in the darkness, their faces delicately lit by the violins, the chorus girls present themselves to the camera one by one. Then the violin-playing girls circle Ruby Keeler. Their hoop dresses seen from above create the image of flower petals, and when they shrink the circle, the image is a flower closing its buds.

The last number, "My Forgotten Man," is one of the earliest examples of social criticism in a musical. "Forgotten Man" was the term applied to World War I veterans who had been hit by the Depression. In 1932 they marched on Washington to demand their war bonus and were forcibly turned away. In this number, a policeman is about to arrest a bum, but stops when Joan Blondell points out his war medal. She sings, "Remember my Forgotten Man, you put a rifle in his hand, you shouted 'hip hooray,' and sent him on his way, but look at him today." This fades into newsreel footage of the soldiers going off to war, and then scenes of a breadline.

Choreographer Busby Berkeley went to obsessive lengths to get the proper shot of his extravaganzas, even boring holes in the roof of his enormous soundstage.

The revolving platform allowed Berkeley to create shifting geometric patterns from the legs of chorus girls.

BABES IN ARMS (1939) is the adolescent version of a backstage musical. It tries to prove that putting on a show is so simple that anyone can do it. This proposition is easy to prove when two of the child stars are Mickey Rooney and Judy Garland.

According to the plot formula of this film (which spawned a series of Mickey/Judy films often called "backyard" musicals), a bunch of kids have to raise money. Everyone ponders this for a few seconds, then suddenly comes up with the idea "Let's put on a show!" They use the barn as a stage and the tractor as a revolving set. The show they put on somehow looks more professional than anything Broadway could do, but that's just part of the fun. In this film, the kids are all actors' children fighting the town busybody who wants to remove them from the corrupt world of show biz and put them all in work schools. The show is intended to prove that show people are okay and that actors are lovable people.

Young Judy Garland is the most lovable of the kids, singing an innocent yet touching rendition of "I Cried for You," for Mickey Rooney. Where Garland is subdued and simple, Rooney is flamboyant and sophisticated, demonstrating his versatility by doing an FDR imitation and then a grotesque blackface song. The minstrel show is one of several strange numbers in the film, including the mindlessly patriotic finale "God's Country," which has guns going off, soldiers marching, the Supreme Court pondering, and everyone proclaiming the beauties of Freedom in America, where "every man is his own dictator." An unintentionally frightening moment is provided by the title song, in which Rooney walks through the town singing, gradually enlisting more and more kids to help him put his show on, until finally his group resembles an angry mob carrying torches.

HOLIDAY INN (1942) is a snappy, funny film that features the first pairing of Bing Crosby and Fred Astaire. Unlikely team that they were, they nonetheless had an amiable chemistry between them. The laid-back Crosby and the sophisticated Astaire casually fight over the same women against a backdrop of show biz and ambition (or lack thereof). Bing runs a nightclub in Connecticut that opens only on national holidays. Bing likes the gimmick because he only has to work eleven days a year; it's a treat for audiences because a new production number is staged for each holiday.

The film starts with a song and dance number featuring Crosby, Astaire, and Virginia Dale. Crosby tries to win the girl with his dancing, while Astaire woos with his singing. Astaire does a good Crosby imitation, although Crosby can't match Astaire's footwork. Offstage there is a similar problem. Crosby wants to retire and marry Dale, but she wants to stay with Astaire and dedicate her life to "making people happy with our feet." Crosby wants peace and quiet, so he decides to open the inn. The inn is successful thanks to a new singing sensation, Marjorie Reynolds, who Crosby discovers by accident. In the meantime Astaire's partner deserts him, so he downs a bottle of Scotch, goes to Connecticut, and does a funny drunk dance with Crosby's new lead singer. There then ensues a new battle for this girl's affection, and Crosby eventually wins.

Because the Holiday Inn has a different floor show for each holiday, Irving Berlin had to stretch to the limit to write appropriate songs. The July 4th segment is downright peculiar. Crosby comes out wearing an Uncle Sam hat as the chorus sings, "Here comes the Freedom Man." But while he sings "Song of Freedom," military film footage is shown, which seems to contradict the sense of freedom. Fred Astaire also does a sparkling solo number, going out on a shiny black floor in casual slacks, doing a casual tap until he smashes a firecracker to the floor with a loud bang. This is the only time Astaire's dance floor was scuffed and marked at the end of a number.

Holiday Inn was such a success that it was followed by **BLUE SKIES** (1946), which was almost a remake. Crosby and Astaire are together again with more Irving Berlin songs and dozens of great numbers. Although Crosby sings "White Christmas" again, he is still no match for Astaire.

Astaire's brilliant dance "Puttin' On the Ritz" is a film-stopping masterpiece. We see Astaire beating out a rhythm with his cane, dropping it to the floor with a smash and dancing on it. Then a mirrored door opens, and he enters a room in which dozens of Fred Astaires are dancing. Astaire continues the cane dance, now echoed by his partners. Astaire in the front drops to one knee and smashes the head of the cane on the floor to the beats of the music. Then Astaire twirls, while the Astaires in the background raise their canes high in counterpoint.

In Summer Stock, *Judy Garland makes the transition from New England farm girl to show-stealing theatrical trouper.*

SUMMER STOCK (1950) is a pleasant variation on a very old theme: actors trying to put on their own show. Although a minor film in the backstage musicals sub-genre, it provides many delights, chiefly due to the performances of Gene Kelly and the original "let's put on a show" girl, Judy Garland.

The central theme of the film is familiar. Judy Garland plays a wholesome farm girl who's perfectly content to be driving a tractor (while singing of course), and Gene Kelly is a wolfish actor who tries to win Garland. They've both played these parts before. While the film provides pleasant entertainment, it rarely rises to the heights one associates with Kelly and Garland. This lethargy is in part attributable to the problems Garland was going through at the time; her previous film had driven her almost to a nervous breakdown, and she started making *Summer Stock* before her rest cure was over.

The highlight of the film, shot months after the rest of *Summer Stock* was completed and after Garland had lost quite a bit of weight, shows Garland's true capability. Garland appears in a man's jacket which barely covers her thighs and a hat sexily tilted over her eye, and belts out "Get Happy" accompanied by four men clapping their hands to the bouncy rhythm. Garland is irresistible, sexier than ever, and in top singing form. This was Garland's last musical number at MGM; it is a triumphant parting shot.

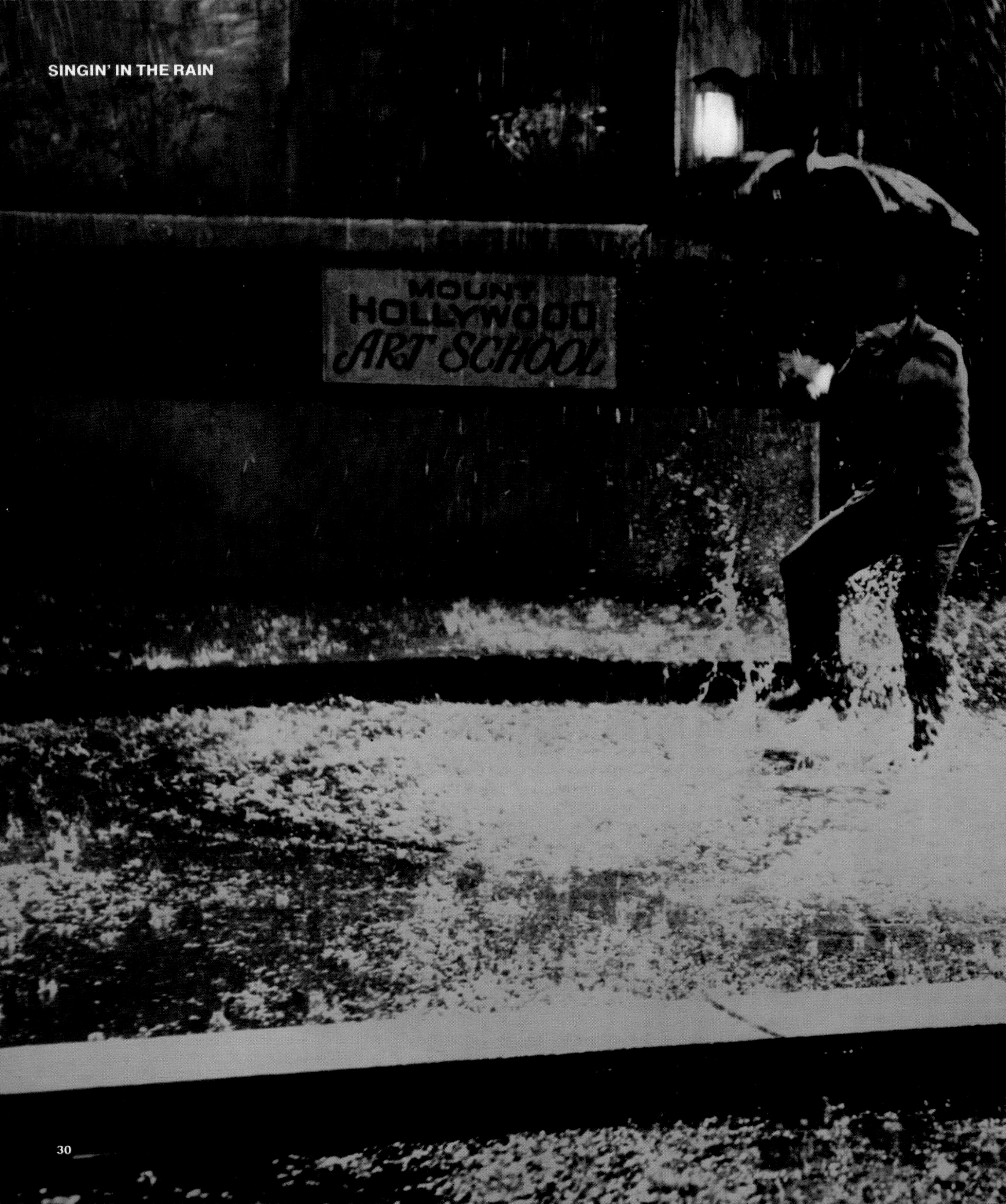
MOUNT
HOLLYWOOD
ART SCHOOL

In the title sequence from Singin' in the Rain, Gene Kelly forever captured the irrepressible joy and flights of controlled abandon possible in a musical. His singing, jumping, splashing, stomping, and dancing in the rain create the high point of a film studded with magical moments.

SINGIN' IN THE RAIN (1952) is a backstage musical with a twist. It is about the making of a movie musical at the most pivotal point in motion picture history: the year sound film was invented. In a sense, *Singin' in the Rain* brings the musical genre full circle, because it is a celebration of the birth of musicals.

The film is about the panic that went through Hollywood when all the underpinnings of the industry were removed. Silent films had been made with a freedom that was not possible in sound films. When silent stars Don Lockwood (Gene Kelly) and Lina Lamont (Jean Hagan) perform for the cameras, it doesn't matter if Lockwood calls Lamont a treacherous rattlesnake under his breath, because the public sees only images of love. But when the same love scene is shot with sound, the production becomes a crisis. The beautiful Lina Lamont has a terrible speaking voice, and the only romantic dialogue Don Lockwood, the heartthrob of millions, can think of is "I love you" (which he repeats incessantly). The soundmen have even more problems. They can't figure out where to put the microphone. They try hiding it in a flowerpot, but every time Lamont turns her head, her voice disappears. Then they sew the mike into her dress, but it picks up her heartbeat, loud and clear. The producer walks in while the soundmen are fuming, yanks a loose wire connected to Lina, and topples her off her chair. Solving these technical problems becomes crucial to the story.

Many of the musical numbers have a behind-the-scenes quality. In "Make 'Em Laugh," a knock 'em-in-the-aisles, belly-laugh number, Donald O'Connor does everything possible to make Gene Kelly laugh. He dodges stage hands moving furniture, gets smacked with a long two-by-four and opens a door fronting on a brick wall and smacks into it. The finale is a rare example of funny musical slapstick. O'Connor

runs into a painted door and, defying gravity, walks up the set and does a complete backflip, a maneuver he repeats until he finally crashes through a fake wall. In "You Were Meant for Me," the power of cinema to create an artificial but beautiful world is revealed. Gene Kelly leads Debbie Reynolds onto an empty stage in order to disclose his love. The setting is just a warehouse until Kelly throws a switch. Then, like magic, a beautiful sunset appears behind them. Kelly flicks another switch which he says adds "mist from distant mountains," and tops it off with a summer breeze supplied by a fan. Using a ladder as a balcony, he tenderly serenades Reynolds. As in movies, the illusion created is more appealing than the real thing.

The film's opening credits serve as both a refrain of the title song and a parody of the revue format of early musicals.

The amazing thing about *Singin' in the Rain* is that every musical number is special, making it hard to single out one as the best. The title song, though, captures the greatest qualities of the film. It transforms the ordinary into the extraordinary through dance and music. After walking Reynolds home, Kelly stands in the rain, thinking about his love. Oblivious to the weather, he strolls down the street. When he finally notices that it is raining, he closes his umbrella with a shrug and continues strolling. In the dance that follows, Kelly turns a drenching rainstorm into a celebration of happiness. As he walks down the street singing, he suddenly jumps up and hangs from a street light. He plays with his umbrella— waltzing with it, twirling it, and

kicking it high into the air and catching it. As the dance becomes more exciting, Kelly spins with his opened umbrella, and then reverts to childhood, stomping in puddles. He stops sheepishly when he discovers a policeman watching him. His only defense is to shrug and sing "I'm dancin' and singin' in the rain." The number is essential Gene Kelly because it depends not only on his athletic dancing, but also his playful nature. The result is a dance that can be watched repeatedly without diminished impact.

The film's climactic ballet, "Broadway Rhythm," is a backstage musical in itself. In this rich and complex number, a fresh-faced kid comes to New York to become a dancer. He works his way to the heights of success, gets involved with a gangster's moll, loses her, and then concludes that dancing is his life. Entire films have been built around less material than this. One of the highpoints occurs in a nightclub. Kelly dances exuberantly with painted silhouettes of people in the background. After a particularly spectacular jump and spin, he drops to his knees and suddenly comes face-to-foot with two of the most beautiful legs in screen history, those of Cyd Charisse. The camera moves up her leg to reveal a cold beauty sitting at a gangster's table. She gets up and seductively dances in front of Kelly, displaying her wares, swinging her hips and sexily blowing smoke into his face. She takes his glasses off, blows on them, wipes them on her thigh, then kicks them away with her heel. Finally fed up, Kelly grabs her and holds her close to him. She melts in his arms and slides to the floor. Before the romance can be consummated, however, the gangster appears, dangling a necklace in front of Charisse's nose. The number bristles with imagination and wit. There is also a little extravaganza-parody involved because the number has nothing to do with anything in *Singin' in the Rain.* It fits only because, like the film, it is brilliant.

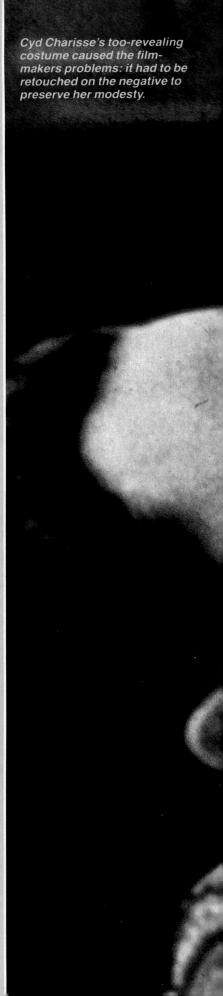

THE BEST OF SHOW BIZ FOLKS

"Let me entertain you,
Let me make you smile. . . ."

"Let Me Entertain You"
Stephen Sondheim and Jule Styne

Martin Scorsese's New York, New York *imaginatively recreates
the Harlem Club, infamous meeting place of the true jazz greats.*

A Star is Born is Hollywood's favorite legend about itself. The story has been made four times so far, including the 1932 original, *What Price Hollywood?*

A STAR IS BORN (1954) features the best film performance of the musical's greatest female star, Judy Garland. The film highlights Garland's acting ability, a facet that was little used in most of her musicals. But there are songs, too, songs which flow powerfully from her performance.

While Judy Garland dominates the film, its other elements are on target as well. *A Star is Born* remains one of the best behind-the-scenes films about the lives and torments of show business people yet made.

The story concerns a Hollywood romance doomed to failure because of the fickle nature of celebrity. Esther Blodgett (Judy Garland) is a hidden talent discovered by the great actor Norman Maine (James Mason). He helps get her career started, marries her,

and she becomes a star. At the same time, Maine's career is ruined by his alcoholism. He watches his wife get famous while he sinks into oblivion. These tensions come to a climax when Blodgett (now renamed Vicki Lester) wins the Academy Award. She's just about to make her acceptance speech when her husband stumbles drunkenly to the podium, musters all the dignity that he can, and begs for a job. Esther tries to restrain him, and he accidentally slaps her.

This is all broadcast on nation-wide television and gives a perfect picture of one celebrity rising and another sinking.

The spectacular "Born in a Trunk" number says more about life on the road in its 18 minutes than most films specifically on the subject. Director George Cukor had to cut 37 minutes from his finished film, including some songs rumored to be among Garland's best, yet the film is still long at 154 minutes. "The Man That

Vicki Lester (Judy Garland) hears the amazing news that she has won the coveted Oscar. Her moment of glory will be ruined by the arrival of her drunken husband, Norman Maine (James Mason), however.

Got Away" was *not* cut, and remains a Garland *tour de force*. Cukor's original version of the film has recently been reconstructed by the Academy of Motion Picture Arts and Sciences.

It is ironic that Judy Garland, who was disovered by MGM at the age of 12 and spent 20 years there nurturing her talents, should have her finest role in a film by Warner Brothers Studio. *A Star is Born* was Garland's last musical film role.

Dorothy Parker wrote the screenplay for the 1937 version of the story, which featured Fredric March and Janet Gaynor. *A Star is Born* was remade as a musical again in 1977 starring Barbra Streisand and Kris Kristofferson. While the two leads are engaging stars with commanding singing styles, this film falls flat. Unlike its predecessor, the remake failed to provide anything more than shallow characterizations and relied heavily on cliché value for storytelling.

NEW YORK, NEW YORK

(1977) is both a tribute to, and a critique of, the musicals of the 1940s. The structure of 1940s musicals is lovingly recreated, and then subverted, by characters who are real people with real problems. The effect is often exhilarating, but just as often irritating. Director Martin Scorsese has never been interested in making "safe" movies, and *New York, New York* is anything but "safe."

As the opening credits roll, the style of the movie is set. First, a New York skyline, dark and beautiful, appears; then the stylish Art Deco title rises over the horizon, mixing the real and the artificial as the 1940s musicals did. The story begins on VJ Day in New York. Musician Jimmy Doyle (Robert DeNiro) spies singer Francine Evans (Liza Minnelli), and tries unsuccessfully to pick her up. He badgers her for her telephone number, leaves, and in classic pick-up style returns to ask "Was that fellow bothering you?" In the fashion of musicals, the two fall in love and marry. Things do not go smoothly, however, because they each have their careers to thrash out. Doyle is egotistical, possessive and jealous. He does not want his wife to have any success, and he mistreats her. Finally they divorce, and each goes it alone.

Scorsese plays his story against stylized sets that would not seem out of place in a Gene Kelly musical. In one scene, Minnelli and DeNiro stand outdoors in a snowbank with a forest of cardboard trees in the background. The ultimate in stylization occurs when DeNiro is at a train station on a set full of snow. As the train pulls out and we see it is a moving piece of paper cardboard with cut-outs for windows, DeNiro grabs hold of it and tries to keep it from leaving. These effects are startling,

Jimmy Doyle (Robert DeNiro) finds the right release for his talent wailing bebop at the Harlem Club. DeNiro's playing style was modeled after well-known bebop musicians.

but Scorsese uses them to add historical texture to his story and to "out-Hollywood" Hollywood.

The one element that Scorsese does not copy from the old musicals is the music itself. There are plenty of songs sung by Minnelli and plenty of jazz arrangements played by DeNiro, but there are no "musical" songs; for example, no one breaks out singing in a restaurant. All of the songs are done in performance settings with no camera tricks. In Minnelli's stirring rendition of the title song she stands on a stage in front of a huge crowd and sings. The focus stays where it should be—on the performer.

The acting in the film is superb, and definitely not out of a 1940s musical. DeNiro is thoroughly obnoxious and convincing as a man who thinks the world revolves around him. When Minnelli deserts him to go on tour, he chases after her. When he finds her, months later, he shouts, "*You* don't say goodbye, *I* say goodbye!" His egotism comes through in every scene.

Minnelli has a more difficult role. She has to make it seem that she likes DeNiro. She almost pulls it off, but she is too strong a character to stay with him as long as she does. While her singing scenes are dynamic, for the most part she has a thankless role.

Although *New York, New York* has problems, they are of a different sort than those of most modern musicals. Scorsese takes away a myth and doesn't replace it with anything. The filmmaker understands the musical genre and what made it great. This understanding gave him the freedom to explore new possibilities for the form.

Liza Minnelli borrowed not only her mother's (Judy Garland's) singing style, but her look and mannerisms as well for this show-stopping rendition of "New York, New York."

Ralph Garcy (Barry Miller) does his Freddie Prinze imitation—both in comic style and personal instability—for his friends in Fame.

Though **FAME** (1980) harks back to the old-fashioned musicals which featured talented kids trying to make it big, its contemporary dialogue, editing, and landscape update it. *Fame* is about New York City's High School of Performing Arts and the people in it. It follows several kids as they audition for the school and progress through four years. Somewhere underneath is a Mickey Rooney/Judy Garland movie struggling to get out.

The film constantly shifts between stories of six young performers. Montgomery (Paul McCrane) is the gay son of a successful actress who is always on the road. Doris Finsucker (Maureen Teefy) is spurred on by a possessive Jewish mother who wants her to be a singer. Ralph Garcy (Barry Miller), a.k.a. Raoul Garcia, is a talented but abrasive comic, uncomfortable with his ghetto background. Bruno (Lee Curreri) is an electronic music genius who does his best work in his basement. He is encouraged by Coco (Irene Cara), a dynamic singer with big ambitions. And LeRoy (Gene Anthony Ray) is a terrific dancer who cannot read.

The editing style gives only key moments in fragmentary scenes from the four years of high school. The technique gives energy and drive to the early scenes, and quickly introduces the characters. Because the film is not centered around any one person, the individual characters never emerge full-blown. Character development often occurs between the scenes, leaving the viewer with only sketchy details about interesting characters. We never find out what Montgomery wants in life, for instance, or why it has taken LeRoy four years to figure out that he won't graduate if he doesn't learn to read.

Several interesting musical numbers give the film an old-fashioned feeling. In the school cafeteria, students start tapping on the tables, others start to dancing to the rhythm, and then the music students (who conveniently have their instruments with them) join in. The scene becomes a huge configuration of bodies writhing within a tight space as the camera isolates bits of choreography—pure musical fantasy. In another number, Bruno's father parks his taxi in front of the school, blaring his son's song "Fame." Suddenly all the kids are in the street dancing—on car tops, on the sidewalk, and through the streets. Both are honest-to-goodness musical production numbers with people breaking out into song for no good reason. The numbers are choreographed to look spontaneous, though of course, they are not. Oscar-winning composer Michael Gore also wrote the script. *Fame* is so flashy, quick, and lively that its small faults are easily overlooked.

Director Alan Parker has a knack for getting exhuberant performances out of young actors, as evidenced in *Bugsy Malone* (1976), *The Wall* (1982), and *Shoot the Moon* (1982).

In 1916, a newspaper article declared: "It may be predicted that the talking picture will never replace the photoplay." This skepticism persisted until Warner Brothers decided to produce **THE JAZZ SINGER** (1927) with Al Jolson.

The plot concerns a cantor's son who deserts the synagogue for the Broadway stage. *The Jazz Singer* conveys a vivid sense of Jewish life. Much of the filming was done in the Jewish ghetto around Orchard Street in New York City. Director Alan Crosland used residents of the area as extras, contributing authenticity to the film. Warner Oland, who plays Jolson's father, later became famous as Charlie Chan. Myrna Loy is also featured in a bit part as a chorus girl.

Al Jolson's unrestrained showmanship is still a one-man embodiment of a whole show business tradition, of performers giving their all to connect with the audience. His "Mammy," *is* American musical comedy. Early in the picture, after completing a number, he cries, "Wait a minute, wait a minute, you ain't heard nothin' yet," and launches into "Toot Toot Tootsie Goodbye." It's an electrifying moment, since Jolson spontaneously improvised the dialogue.

Years later, the movie inevitably shows its age. The technical aspects are primitive, the story grossly sentimental. Two other *Jazz Singers* have been made (Danny Thomas in 1952 and Neil Diamond in 1980), but neither comes close to the quality of the original. By comparison, both remakes feel synthetic. Danny Thomas lacks Jolson's charisma, and Peggy Lee is unconvincing as the girl he loves. Version three features an over-age Neil Diamond and a hammy Laurence Olivier, plus a score that never suggests jazz, Jewish culture, or anything except a desire to hit the charts.

New York City's High School of Performing Arts is glamorized in classic Hollywood fashion in Fame.

The team of Fred Astaire and Ginger Rogers reunited, ten years after breaking up, in **THE BARKLEYS OF BROADWAY** (1949). The film tries to recapture their old formula of romantic feuding and inevitable reconciliation. The film doesn't compare with the best of their earlier films, but it is delightful and has its magical moments.

The Barkleys are a famous Broadway dancing team who specialize in light romantic comedy, allowing Astaire and Rogers to play themselves (or at least the Hollywood image of themselves). True to the events of ten years earlier, Mrs. Barkley wants to break up the team so that she can work in serious drama. (Ginger Rogers was in some excellent melodramas including *Stage Door* and *Kitty Foyle*). The film deals with the Barkley's attempts to survive and to reunite.

They do reunite, of course. And along the way they perform some excellent solo and duet songs and dances. The highlights are "Shoes with Wings On," one of Astaire's attempts to continue his dancing career without a partner (this time as a shoemaker in a skit where he dances with his entire stock of shoes), and "They Can't Take That Away From Me," a beautiful ballad that facilitates the reunion and is a sort of unofficial theme song of the legend of Fred Astaire and Ginger Rogers.

SWING TIME (1936) is one of the best of the Fred Astaire-Ginger Rogers films. The film makes great use of their special chemistry, both on the dance floor and in the love scenes. In addition to the magnificent dances, the songs bristle as well, with music by Jerome Kern and lyrics by Dorothy Fields. *Swing Time* is a good time.

Fred and Ginger play a professional dance team who bicker and spar with each other until, of course, they fall in love. The plot follows them as they continuously get engaged, always to the wrong people. They embroil themselves in complications without ever straying too far from a solution. The extremely romantic nature of their relationship calls for such slight teasing; no real antagonism can enter their idyllic world.

Fred Astaire and Ginger Rogers regain their old magic when they dance together.

Astaire, a gambler, accidentally meets and infuriates Rogers; he then becomes so infatuated with her that he follows her to the dance studio where she works. Astaire takes a lesson from her and he's terrible. Rogers concludes that he'll never be a dancer. The studio manager (Eric Blore) hears this and fires her. To salvage her job, Astaire shows just what Rogers taught him, to the tune of "Pick Yourself Up." The dance floor cannot contain them in their excitement, and they vault over its railing and back again. In "The Way You Look Tonight," which won an Academy Award as best song, the joke is that while Astaire is singing how beautiful Rogers is, she is washing her hair. Yet with the soap on her head perfectly arranged, she manages to look even more beautiful than usual.

Astaire's best solo number is "Bojangles of Harlem"— his tribute to Bill Robinson.

Astaire is introduced in blackface, on a pair of ten-foot long legs. He does a hot dance with the chorus girls, but the only one who can keep up with Astaire is Astaire, so three silhouettes of himself appear. Astaire dances a dizzying counterpoint to his shadows, outdoing himself, until finally the shadows throw their hands up in disgust and give up.

The final song comes when all seems lost. Rogers is going to marry someone else because she thinks Astaire is going to marry his girlfriend. Sadly Rogers asks Astaire, "Does she dance very beautifully . . .the girl you're in love with?" He answers, "Yes, very." She asks, "The girl you're engaged to?" And he says, "Oh, I don't know. I've danced with you. I'm never going to dance again." In song he explains that because he's lost "La belle, la perfectly swell romance, never gonna dance." The ensuing dance routine, however, proves otherwise. The dance starts out as a sad one, with Astaire's entire body pleading with Rogers, his hands drooping, his head hung down. Then when she is about to leave he grabs her, the music changes tempo, and they do a lively dance with complicated jumps and twists, showing that they love each other.

THE GANG'S ALL HERE
(1943) is a lively film that combines Alice Faye, Carmen Miranda, Busby Berkeley's choreography, and the Benny Goodman Orchestra. Benny's band provides most of the music. Alice Faye provides the languid romantic lead in a slim plot about love intrigues in a tropical nightclub. Carmen Miranda provides the tropical flavor. And Busby Berkeley provides the major reason for wanting to see this film.

Busby Berkeley tops himself here with the most bizarre dance number ever recorded. It is built around Carmen Miranda, a Latin American singer best known for her mangling of English and for her headpieces made out of fruit. Miranda's greatest moment on film is "The Lady With the Tutti Fruitti Hat."

Sigmund Freud once said, "Sometimes a cigar is just a cigar." But to Busby Berkeley, a banana is never just a banana. The phallic overtones of this dance are not missed by anyone past puberty.

The number starts innocently enough as a nightclub act. An organ grinder stands in the audience while his monkey runs away and lands in a banana tree on the stage. Dozens of scantily clad native girls loll around. Suddenly, Miranda makes her entrance on a banana boat. She is wearing a hat made of bananas and strawberries. She also has strawberries glued to the side of her face and her dress. After an interlude on a xylophone that has bananas instead of keys, the number starts to get weird.

The Gang's All Here.

The native girls, wearing yellow bloomers and loose black tops, grab four-foot bananas and run wild. The girls hug the bananas and thrust them up and down in the air in such an obviously phallic fashion that it is a wonder the number made it past the censors. The girls line up, hold their fruit out, and create a rolling wave of bananas. To get the full effect, the camera tilts and constantly changes perspective, shooting from above and below. The final shot focuses on Miranda singing while the camera slowly pulls back. Her headdress of bananas grows taller and taller until it touches the ceiling. The headpiece seems to stretch into infinity, but actually it was only 30 feet high.

THREE LITTLE WORDS (1950) must have given audiences pause at first. A musical about Bert Kalmar and Harry Ruby? Yet these obscure songwriters provided the basis for the best musical biography ever made.

Kalmar and Ruby were Tin Pan Alley songwriters who specialized in such comic songs as "Hooray for Captain Spaulding" and "I Wanna Be Loved By You" (Betty Boop's anthem). They wrote all of the Marx

Brothers' memorable tunes. In terms of accurately portraying the team, Fred Astaire and Red Skelton (who play Bert Kalmar and Harry Ruby, respectively) are ridiculously miscast. Kalmar and Ruby were two very Jewish songwriters. But one never expects the whole truth from Hollywood, and *Three Little Words* captures the spirit of Kalmar and Ruby remarkably.

Astaire's Kalmar begins his career as a dancer. His secret love, though, is magic. His dancing and his magic go bust and he takes to songwriting. Skelton's Ruby also has an outside interest. He loves baseball. These little peccadilloes give life to the characters. In other musical biographies, the subjects usually live, eat, and breathe their work, but Bert Kalmar and Harry Ruby are believable as real people. The film anecdotally recounts various incidents in their career. In one memorable scene, the two walk along the street arguing about a tune. They see a piano being moved into a house and stop to play on it. They sing "I Wanna Be Loved By You." Suddenly, a breezy flapper (Debbie Reynolds in her first film) strolls by and supplies the squeaky "boop boop a doop." While this may not have been how the song was written, it does show them working. Most other composer's biographies ignore the process of creation.

The film succeeds because it is loose and relaxed. Director Richard Thorpe went on the assumption that Kalmar and Ruby did not warrant a reverential tone. *Three Little Words* is the best tribute MGM could have given to two of the quirkiest composers who ever lived.

The lives of show people usually furnish a flimsy excuse to wrap some backstage clichés around a musical score. **SHOWBOAT** is one of the outstanding exceptions. It has flesh and blood characters that live and breathe and reach out to modern audiences. In 1936, Universal presented a widely-acclaimed version starring Irene Dunne and Allan

Jones, and MGM remade it in color with Howard Keel and Kathryn Grayson in 1951.

The 1936 film is darker and more melodramatic. British director James Whale coaxed sensitive performances from his entire cast. Irene Dunne is appealing as Magnolia, daughter of Cap'n Andy (Charles Winninger), who runs the showboat. Her romance with gambler Gaylord Ravenal (Allan Jones) provides the main conflict. Helen Morgan is touching as Julie, the unfortunate mulatto who loses her man when he discovers her mixed blood.

The Kern-Hammerstein songs are classics. Most memorable of all is Paul Robeson's spine-chilling "Old Man River." This moment projects all the pathos of lost hope and makes one regret again the neglect of Robeson's talents by Hollywood.

The 1951 production of *Showboat* is glossier. Howard Keel is a physical and vocal match for Allan Jones as the dashing Ravenal, and Ava Gardner's Julie is surprisingly touching. Her voice is dubbed—unfairly, since her singing on the hit soundtrack is superior to the voice MGM forced her to use in the film.

Kathryn Grayson's Magnolia doesn't live up to the standard set by Dunne. She's too kittenish, her soprano too piercing. Marge and Gower Champion contribute lively dance routines. Joe E. Brown is an amusing Cap'n Andy. William Warfield's "Old Man River" is stirring, though it lacks the raw power Robeson supplies.

Both *Showboats* are impressively mounted and ably directed, but only the first achieves classic status.

RHYTHM ON THE RIVER (1940) is a jaundiced look at the insidious world of show business. This tale of an abused songwriting team, though considerably lightened by its romantic tone, reflects a cynical view of theatrical ethics.

The film presents Broadway songwriter Oliver Courtney (Basil Rathbone), who writes neither words nor lyrics. Bob Summers (Bing Crosby) writes the music and Cherry Lane (Mary Martin) writes the lyrics. The two do not know about each other at first, but meet on a writing vacation at the same resort. They discover that they've been collaborating long distance and conclude that Courtney is taking advantage of them. Summers and Lane dump Courtney and try to make it on their own, but they are caught in a catch-22 situation. Ironically, publishers reject their songs because they sound like Oliver Courtney imitations.

The story gives Crosby and Martin ample opportunity to sing. With jazzy orchestrations, these scenes have real pep. In terms of image, Crosby has never been better. He is completely lackadaisical, smoking his pipe and making it seem an effort to move. His only aspiration in life is to sit on a boat in the river and fish, which is where the title of the film comes from. Mary Martin is fresh and engaging in this, one of her few screen appearances. Basil Rathbone is particularly unctious as the unscrupulous villain. He lives with his "secretary," Oscar Levant, and they always bicker. Levant was a great wit, and his sour countenance fits right in.

Stormy Weather.

STORMY WEATHER (1943) is a rare black musical from a major studio, 20th Century Fox. Sometimes condescending, it nonetheless contains some of the most amazing individual performances ever recorded on film, and therefore deserves serious consideration.

Stormy Weather is allegedly about the life of Bill "Bojangles" Robinson, the black dancer who actually made a career for himself in Hollywood at a time when blacks only played domestics and slaves. Robinson succeeded as a sort of compromise candidate. He was a gifted performer, but his acting often adopted stereotyped mannerisms: an Uncle Tom laugh, a permanent empty-faced grin, and perpetually wide eyes. The other star of the film is Lena Horne. In contrast to Robinson, Horne refused to do any stereotyped roles; as a result she wasn't in many films.

The story begins in 1917. Bill Robinson comes back from World War I, meets Lena Horne, and then leaves to pursue his career. They meet again, after finding success. Robinson wants to marry and settle down, but Horne doesn't, because they're show people and always on the move. They split up again, only to be reunited at the finale.

The film is slowly paced, there is no conflict, and the musical numbers really do not relate to the plot. What the musical numbers *do* do is give Horne ample opportunity to sing. She does wonderful renditions of "Diga Diga Doo" and "I Can't Give You Anything But Love Baby." Her big production number is "Stormy Weather," in which she is excellent.

Robinson only gets a few opportunities to dance, but he is good, too. The supporting singers and dancers nearly steal the film. Cab Calloway and his band perform brilliantly. Fats Waller appears briefly to give the definitive version of "Ain't Misbehavin'." The Nicholas Brothers, an incredible tap dancing team, perform the finale. They tap-dance on a wide stairway, leaping over each other with every move. They may be the world's fastest tap dancers, and are certainly the most athletic.

Stormy Weather is a frustrating film because it is so extreme. It is both excellent and horrible.

This Caribbean dance from Stormy Weather is typical of the stereotyping that weakens the whole film.

GYPSY (1962) is a great tale of the show biz life. Perfectly integrating story and song, and set in the years when vaudeville faded to burlesque, the plot follows the stormy but strong relationship of a stage mother and her young daughter. The girl grows up to be the greatest stripper of her time. While the tale could have easily been made dirty and embarrassing, the intelligence of the performers and the filmmakers gives *Gypsy* a lot of class.

This musical fable is a twisted success story. Madame Rose is an archetypal stage mother. Domineering and pushy, all she wants is for her daughters to succeed on the stage. The act is centered around Baby June, while her ugly duckling sister Louise is hidden away in a cow suit. They keep performing the same routines until Baby June deserts the act. Then Rose forces Louise into the star spot, but vaudeville is dying. At an especially low point, they accept a booking at a burlesque house, and when the star stripper doesn't show up, Rose sends Louise out to strip in front of a crowd of drooling men. The newly named Gypsy Rose Lee is an astounding success and makes it to the top of the field, taking Momma with her.

Natalie Wood gives her all in Gypsy. *Though she delivered stellar performances as both the stripteasing Louise, and as Maria in* West Side Story *from the previous year, Natalie Wood never made another musical.*

Gypsy is based on the life of stripper Gypsy Rose Lee, whose sister is June Havoc. Ethel Merman played Madame Rose on Broadway, and eyebrows were raised when Rosalind Russell got the movie role. But Russell is surprisingly good, alternately fierce and loving, demanding and understanding. She does not try to match Merman's singing; in fact, her songs were partially dubbed in by Lisa Kirk.

Karl Malden is adequate as Herbie, Rose's love, and fortunately has only one song. The surprise in the film is Natalie Wood as Louise, emerging from a dumpy awkward girl into a stunningly beautiful woman in seconds. Her strip scenes are tasteful yet sensual.

Gypsy.

The most striking thing about *Gypsy* are the incisive songs, written by Stephen Sondheim and Jule Styne. They deftly interweave character and plot development. Early in the film, Rose sings "Some People," which reveals her feeling that she cannot take joy in ordinary life. Later, when she meets a man she would like to latch onto, they sing "Small World," not exactly a love song. It makes the point that Rose does not have room for true love, but she can be tender. Rose's final climactic number is "Rose's Turn"; she finally takes center stage and reveals her ambitions, her disappointments, and the fact that she has lived her life through her daughters.

The songs provide a dramatic unity to the film, which is especially important because it takes place over a span of several years. Early in the film Baby June sings the song, "Let Me Entertain You," which has lines like "I can do a few tricks, some old and then some new tricks, I'm very versatile." The same song is used when Gypsy Rose Lee does her strip act, but it takes on a completely new meaning. Other links are provided by the songs in Baby June's routines. No matter how Rose dresses up the act, it is still the same through the years, a point made by using variations on the same tune.

Gypsy is not without flaws. The first half drags in parts, although the contrast doubles the impact of the lively strip scene. The story is ultimately very moving, and the film is a classic of musical drama.

In **FUNNY GIRL** (1968), Barbra Streisand brilliantly impersonates Fanny Brice, a multi-talented actress, singer, and comedienne. The story of Brice's professional success is a natural for the screen.

The film opens with an elegantly dressed Brice passing a mirror and saying, in a mock Jewish accent, "Hello, gorgeous." In that one moment, she reveals herself as both the superstar and the girl who cannot believe her luck. Brice considers herself funny-looking and so constantly jokes about her appearance. In flashbacks to Brice's home on New York's Lower East Side, the reasons for her self-image become clear. Brice's mother (Kay Medford) and her friends pick each other apart with humor. Mae Questel, the voice of Betty Boop, sings that Brice cannot be a star because her "incidentals aren't bigger than two lentils." But Brice doesn't lack confidence, and she pursues a show business career.

She is quickly cast in the Ziegfield Follies, but then she rebels. The Follies' finale is a bridal number proclaiming Brice's beauty. She asks to bow out of the number, contending that "they'll laugh at me." Ziegfield, however, is adamant, so she appears on opening night playing the beautiful bride and singing all the songs—but she appears to be nine months pregnant. Brice brings the house down as she sings "I am the beautiful reflection of my love's affection."

The cast is excellent. Omar Sharif as Brice's suitor (and then husband) Nicky Arnstein is handsome and cool. Kay Medford claims some of the best dialogue in the picture: when Sharif shows up at a beer party, Streisand says, "A gentleman fits in anyplace," and Medford retorts, "A sponge fits in anyplace!"

But the film belongs to Streisand. In a *tour de force* movie debut, she reveals herself as a talented comedienne, a brilliant singer, and a vibrant screen personality. She even does slapstick. She also has her share of touching and funny songs by Bob Merrill and Jule Styne. The big hit was "People," but her performance of "Don't Rain On My Parade" is even better.

The scenes of Brice performing are terrific, and the first half of the film sparkles. But when Nicky Arnstein, a gambler who cannot control himself, shows up, she marries him, and the film slows down. There have been hundreds of stories told about a woman loving a man who is no good, and almost as many about a man who cannot accept his wife's success. So *Funny Girl* is a mixed blessing. If there had been more Fanny Brice and less Nicky Arnstein, it would have been a true classic. It alternately soars and plummets, but when it soars, it's really something.

Show-biz show-off Joe Gideon (Roy Scheider) turns his death into a production number. Here, he and Ben Vereen dance with the corpuscle girls. All That Jazz also contains scenes where Gideon waxes philosophical with the Angel of Death (Jessica Lange), a clear echo of Fellini's 8½.

Few show business people have bared their souls as much as Bob Fosse does in **ALL THAT JAZZ** (1979). He presents an unflattering portrait of himself, one acknowledging not only his talent, but also his excesses. The film, like Fosse, walks a tightrope between talent and excess.

All That Jazz is clearly about Bob Fosse; the striking parallels between his life and career and those of Joe Gideon (played by Roy Scheider) cannot be glossed over. Joe Gideon is directing a stage show which looks suspiciously like "Chicago" (which Fosse directed). In addition, Gideon's ex-wife is in his musical, as Fosse's (Gwen Verdon) was in "Chicago." He is in the process of editing a film that looks suspiciously like *Lenny* (a Bob Fosse film), and lives with dancer Ann Reinking, Fosse's one-time real-life roommate.

The private lives of creative people, such as this million-dollar choreographer, hold a certain voyeuristic interest, but the film really lights up whenever there is a dance. "Everything Old is New Again" is a relaxed soft-shoe number performed by Gideon's mistress and his daughter. Gideon choreographs a spectacular celebration of sex for the show he is directing, a stylized orgy set to music. The most elaborate stunts are saved for the end. Gideon is dying. Suddenly, Ben Vereen appears as a master of ceremonies and sings "Bye Bye Life." Other people appear, including dancers dressed like blood vessel anatomy models and guitarists in silver death masks. The exuberant dance that follows goes on for a long time. When Gideon finally dies, the film ends on a strangely upbeat note.

The problem with the film is that there is no discipline to Fosse's revelations about himself and thus, while he shows everything, he reveals nothing. Even with Fosse's lapses in judgment, *All That Jazz* is one of the more interesting and flashy musicals of the 1970s.

THE BEST OF AMERICANA

James Cagney as the patriotic George M. Cohan proclaims himself a Yankee Doodle Boy. Cagney gave the performance of his career in *Yankee Doodle Dandy*.

"I like the shores of America, Comfort is yours in America, Knobs on the doors in America, Wall to wall floors in America."

"America"

MEET ME IN ST. LOUIS (1944) is director Vincente Minnelli's masterpiece of nostalgia, presenting turn-of-the-century America through cracked, rose-tinted glasses. In an unforced episodic style, the film attempts to show the timeless joys and pains of a 'typical' family. The year is 1903, a time of small town values and fiercely protective nuclear families. It is the time of the St. Louis Fair, and the whole town is abuzz. The portrait of the Smith family is representative of all of St. Louis, all of mid-America. From the opening scene, in which they sing "Meet Me in St. Louis" together, to the end, the Smiths are presented as a closely-knit and loving family. The film recounts some of the major events in their lives in that fateful year, revealing each family member and showing their growth into stronger people.

Mother (Mary Astor) is making ketchup when Esther (Judy Garland) arrives with the news that sister Rose (Lucille Bremer) is expecting a long distance telephone call from her boyfriend in New York, and that can only mean a proposal. Dinner, therefore, must be served an hour early, as the only phone in the house is in the dining room.

When Alonzo (Leon Ames), the father, comes home from his law office, he refuses to allow the dinner to be changed. So when the phone call comes, the whole family listens as Rose and her boyfriend shout at each other cross-country, and all know that there has been no proposal.

The film is full of memorable touching sequences. Esther, who fell in love at first sight with boy-next-door John Truett (Tom Drake), invites him to a party. He is the last one to leave because he can't find his hat. Esther offers to look for it, runs to the kitchen, and pulls it out of the breadbox, saying casually on her return that it was just where she thought. Now she is alone with John. At her prompting, he helps her turn out the lights in the house, and they walk around snuffing out wicks as the rooms become darker and more romantic, leading almost to the inevitable. But this is 1903, and he doesn't make a move.

Judy Garland sings out her love to the passengers in "The Trolley Song."

Faithful to its small-town ethic, Esther Smith (Judy Garland) finds true love with the boy-next-door, John Truett (Tom Drake), in Meet Me in St. Louis.

The most exceptional scenes in the film concern the ghoulish youngest daughter Tootie (Margaret O'Brien), including the justly famous Halloween episode. Tootie and Esther, suitably costumed, join in the Halloween fun, which involves throwing flour on people they don't like. Tootie is deserted by her sister because she is too young. Tootie seizes the chance to prove herself, and goes to the house of the evil Mr. Brokoff. Mortified with fear, she manages to flour his dog.

In a richly detailed way, the film also recounts how Rose is reconciled with her boyfriend and the trauma that strikes the family when Alonzo announces that he is moving the family to New York—the worst fate imaginable for this family that so loves St. Louis. Tootie's other classic sequence occurs on Christmas Eve. She has just spent the day making snowmen, and she sits with Esther talking about leaving for New York. Esther says that she'll have to leave the snow people behind because they'd melt on the train. Suddenly the reality of leaving St. Louis sinks in, and Tootie rushes into the snow in her nightgown and ferociously smashes her creations. If she can't have them, no one can.

The songs, mostly by Hugh Martin and Ralph Blane, mesh nicely with the story. Esther reveals her love for John Truett early in the film in "The Boy Next Door," but the most famous sequence is "The Trolley Song." Esther waits at the trolley (which goes "clang clang clang") for John Truett, but he does not come, and she boards alone. The chorus starts the song, but every so often the camera cuts to Esther sadly looking out on the street. Suddenly she sees Truett running to catch the car. Only then does Esther join in the song with a burst of happy energy. Later Esther is Garland at her most tender with "Have Yourself a Merry Little Christmas," a touching and ironic song.

The film is full of Vincente Minnelli trademarks—a lush, unrealistic use of technicolor and many charming moments. The family sits at the dinner table awaiting the father when suddenly the sound of someone falling down a flight of steps is heard. The camera tracks across the table, finally resting on Tootie, who says "Now I remember where I left that other skate."

When high-roller Sky Masterson goes down to Havana, he and his Salvation Army girl see this lighter-than-air nightclub floor show.

Marlon Brando proves that method acting alone cannot conquer song and dance in his role as Sky Masterson.

Before MGM made **GUYS AND DOLLS** (1955) into a successful film, the stage show had already been established as one of the greatest Broadway musicals. A flashy and slick tale of gamblers and nightclub singers in love is set against the backdrop of a dream New York. The greatest aspect of the film is the lovable way in which Damon Runyon's characters are brought to life. This New York underworld of gangsters and gamblers isn't threatening in the least; without glamorizing them, the film manages to bring these outlaws of folklore into mainstream culture. The film ver-

sion is faithful to the play. It is lively and enjoyable, though not the classic it might have been, due to some questionable casting choices (a singing Marlon Brando?).

The story concerns Nathan Detroit, a gambler who has two problems: he needs $1000 to buy a place for the big crap game he runs, and Adelaide, his fiancee of fourteen years, is getting impatient about setting a wedding date. Detroit hears that Sky Masterson, a high roller, is in town. When Masterson makes the boast that he can pick up any "Doll" and spend the night with her,

Detroit makes him bet on it, and then picks Sarah Brown of the Salvation Army as the "Doll." Masterson woos Brown, falls in love with her, and marries her in a double ceremony, with Nathan and Adelaide as the other couple.

Jean Simmons as Salvation Army "Doll" Sarah Brown is good at being reserved and unobtainable, and Stubby Kaye as Nicely Johnson (recreating his Broadway performance) has two show-stopping numbers—"Fugue for Tinhorn" and "Sit Down You're Rockin' the Boat"—which he belts out in a sharp

Broadway style. But Vivian Blaine (also from the stage show) gives the best performance as Adelaide, who has a variety of psychosomatic illnesses as a result of "waiting around for that plain little band of gold." She is cunning, disarming, and very funny. Frank Sinatra plays Nathan Detroit, but he walks through the role uninterested in what is happening around him. One problem in the film was the total miscasting of Marlon Brando as Sky Masterson. He was signed up without anyone checking whether he could sing. He recorded the songs for the film over and over again, but was

unable to come up with one complete good take of any of them; the songs in the film result from a splicing together of the better portions from each recording.

Still, it is a fun movie. The songs, written by Frank Loesser—"The Oldest Established Permanent Floating Crap Game," "If I Were a Bell," "Take Back Your Mink," "Sue Me," and "Luck Be a Lady"— are all classics. The dancing, staged by Michael Kidd, is very Broadway, and the jokes still work. *Guys and Dolls* could have been a classic, instead of being just good.

BYE BYE BIRDIE (1963) is a time capsule of a musical that both records and satirizes the early 1960s. It touches on Elvis Presley, small town America, the Cold War, teenagers, and even Ed Sullivan. *Bye Bye Birdie* portrays an innocent time in transition. The kids in this middle American town have Flintstone dolls, go to malt shops, and worry about getting pinned; at the same time they worship a sleazy, sexy, beer-drinking, motorcycle-driving singer loosely based on Elvis Presley. Even respectable people worship Conrad Birdie. When he makes his triumphant entrance walking under an archway of guitars, Birdie sings "Honestly, Sincere," and the whole town faints.

The film opens with the momentous news that Birdie has been drafted into the Army. The news is a blow to girls around the world, but hardest hit is songwriter Albert (Dick Van Dyke), who was just about to have Conrad record his song "Mumbo Jumbo Gooey Gumbo." Albert plans to use the royalties to marry his secretary Rosie (Janet Leigh). Inspired by desperation, Rosie comes up with a plan to have Birdie give a goodbye kiss to all of America on the Ed Sullivan Show. One girl will be chosen randomly to receive said kiss, Birdie will sing Albert's song "One Last Kiss," and it will be a hit.

Ann-Margret.

The chosen girl is Kim MacAfee (Ann-Margret), from Sweet Apple, Ohio. She is a typical teenager, first seen gabbing on the telephone. She has just been pinned by her boyfriend Hugo. In "The Telephone Hour" the news goes from phone to phone with kids in cars, malt shops, beach

Onna White was responsible for the imaginative and exuberant choreography in Bye Bye Birdie. In "A Lot of Livin' to Do," Kim (Ann-Margret) and Hugo try to make each other jealous.

showers, and bubble baths all on the telephone. Hugo (Bobby Rydell) and Kim's father (Paul Lynde) are furious about the kiss. Hugo becomes so jealous that when the show is aired he hits Birdie before Kim's kiss. The song is a disaster, and Albert decides to give up music, become a chemist, and marry Rosie.

The performers in the film are all superb. Dick Van Dyke, repeating his Broadway role, gives one of his most controlled performances, taking a straight part and making it interesting. Janet Leigh works well as a frustrated woman, interested in business and Albert. Maureen Stapleton, as Albert's mother, gives the definitive clinging Jewish mother portrait, from her costume (a mink coat and squeaking golashes) to her lines ("a mother doesn't need food"). Paul Lynde, also from the show, is as acerbic and repressed as ever. But the true delight in the film is Ann-Margret—beautiful, sexy, and alluring.

The songs by Charles Strouse and Lee Adams are wonderful. "Put On a Happy Face" is a sprightly number in which Dick Van Dyke dances a soft shoe with a double exposure of Janet Leigh. "A Lot of Livin' to Do" is an exciting song, performed by dozens of gyrating teenagers as Hugo and Kim try to make each other jealous. Perhaps the most well-known song from the film is "Kids," an amusing litany of parental complaints, sung by Albert's mother and Kim's father.

Bye Bye Birdie shows how much America has changed. The show opened in 1960 and the movie was released only months before John Kennedy's assassination. In the years that followed a true generation gap opened, making a song like "Kids" seem tame by comparison. So Bye Bye Birdie is not only entertaining, but it also has an unintended role as a portrait of an America long gone.

SEVEN BRIDES FOR SEVEN BROTHERS (1954) harks back to the pioneer days of the American West, when early settlers were long on bad manners and short on women folk. They longed for the quiet refinement of marriage and families, but were unaware of the process or the price. *Seven Brides for Seven Brothers* shows the transformation—in song and unbounded dance —of gruff mountain men into loving and gentle husbands.

Howard Keel, the eldest of seven brothers, treks down the mountain and miraculously snares himself a perfect wife in Jane Powell. He has such an easy time that his siblings think that their own matrimonial ambitions will be similarly fulfilled. However, when they find that *their* intendeds want to be courted properly, they are thrown for a loop. Remembering the tale of the "Sobbin' Women" (the Rape of the Sabine women) from Roman history, they decide to kidnap their girls. An avalanche of snow cuts the girls off from rescue, and the boys have the entire winter season to win the hearts of the furious suitees. The feuding boys and girls court and fall in love in spite of themselves.

There are plenty of riotous comic scenes involving Jane Powell's attempts to teach the brothers manners. Her good cooking gives her tremendous leverage over them. But above all, what marks *Seven Brides for Seven Brothers* as exceptional is its exuberant dancing.

Seven Brides for Seven Brothers is a true dance musical. The breathtaking ensemble dances staged by Michael Kidd have never been equalled. The setting allows for some rough and tumble choreography. The best is when the boys go to a barn-raising and see the girls for the first time. They try to impress the girls by cartwheeling out onto the floor, doing handstands, and twirling their partners around. There is an exciting sequence in which

the boys dance on a thin wooden beam a few feet off the ground, jumping from foot to foot while boys from rival families fall off; the absolute topper occurs when one of the brothers takes a hatchet and swings it under his feet during every jump. This dance is ideally suited for the time and place.

GOOD NEWS (1947) is frivolous entertainment at its best. This film version of the 1920s play about college life contains no serious thought and little connection with reality. What's left is a pleasant story, good songs, and great production numbers.

The story is set at Tate College in the 1920s. People say things like "the bees knees" and "23-skidoo." Peter Lawford plays the captain of the football team and the b.m.o.c. (big man on campus). June Allyson plays Connie, a coed in love with Lawford. He ignores Allyson and has eyes set on the beautiful, mysterious and allegedly French Pat McClennan (Patricia Marshall).

The musical numbers are wonderful. In "The Varsity Drag," a gym full of students demonstrates the complexities of the dance. Peter Lawford, though not a great singer, does a nice rendition of "The Best Things in Life Are Free," in French. "Lucky in Love" is sung by everyone on campus, but the best number is "Pass That Peace Pipe," belted out by Joan McCracken. In a malt shop with crowds of kids in college letter shirts, McCracken does an energetic dance, her long legs flying and spinning, while the chorus beats out a tom-tom rhythm and finally joins in dancing while sipping ice cream sodas. Now that's what college should be like!

A gifted singer, dancer, and songwriter, George M. Cohan dominated the early twentieth century with great songs like "You're a Grand Old Flag," "Give My Regards to Broadway," "Over There," and

"Yankee Doodle Dandy." He was the first entertainer to give Americans a sense of themselves as a great people. And indeed, George M. Cohan was himself a great American. When Hollywood decided to honor him by telling his life story, they went all out. They made a great film, starring one of their finest actors.

James Cagney considered his portrayal of George M. Cohan in **YANKEE DOODLE DANDY** (1942) to be his best screen role. It was the most challenging part of his career, and he met the challenge admirably.

Cagney's Cohan will do anything to succeed, and in a sense is a variation on the same character that Cagney played in his gangster films—a gutsy, no-nonsense man, full of self-confidence, grabbing for the American Dream.

While Cagney is great at portraying Cohan the man, he is even better at showing Cohan the performer. All of his numbers are superb. He proves himself a spectacular tap dancer, leaning more towards the Gene Kelly school of athletic dancing than to the Fred Astaire school of grace.

Yankee Doodle Dandy features Cagney in his only Oscar-winning performance. It is ironic that the man who made a career for himself acting as a gangster should receive his highest accolade in an uncharacteristic role.

Fred Astaire and Judy Garland stroll exuberantly down the avenue of show business nostalgia in **EASTER PARADE** (1948). The film explores the struggle between small town values and theatrical ambitions through the story of the rise of an ingenue played by Garland. In the process there is much wonderful singing, dancing, and affectionate interplay.

Judy Garland plays Hannah Brown, a chorus girl from Michigan who has moved to

New York City to make it big in vaudeville. Seasoned pro Don Hewes (Fred Astaire) spots her and helps to develop her career and her heart. The show business aspect of the story allows a steady stream of great tunes to fill the air, while the love story is pleasantly fulfilled through rivalries with extra partners Peter Lawford and Ann Miller.

The film has so many great dances it is hard to single them out, but the two best appear back to back. In "A Couple of Swells," Garland and Astaire come out in tramp costumes, each with a torn coat, missing teeth, and a slight beard. It is simple and direct, structured like a vaudeville number, with two funny tramps trying to act uppercrust. Astaire follows this with a spectacular dance to "Stepping Out with My Baby." Wearing a white suit with red shirt and socks, he starts out doing a fairly standard "Fred Astaire" routine, dancing up and down steps and playing with his cane. But then, for the finale, he dances with his cane in slow motion, while the chorus in the background dances at normal speed.

Easter Parade uses the songs from the entire career of Irving Berlin to provide a rich span of musical history. Classics from previous generations were matched with new works that Berlin had written specifically for the film. The range of music creates a continuity that powerfully expresses the time span of Hannah Brown's career.

Easter Parade was originally to have co-starred Judy Garland and Gene Kelly. Kelly injured himself, and Fred Astaire came out of retirement to make *Easter Parade*. Subsequently he entered the most artistically productive period of his life, and for that we owe *Easter Parade* a deep sense of gratitude. The chance teaming of Garland and Astaire was magical; Astaire's cool professionalism works well with Garland's natural talent.

The Pontipee Brothers (minus eldest brother Howard Keel) with their new sister-in-law, Jane Powell, in *Seven Brides for Seven Brothers. The brothers are:* Jeff Richards, Russ Tamblyn, Tommy Rall, Marc Platt, Matt Mattox, and Jacques D'Amboise.

OKLAHOMA! (1955) is a double dose of Americana. It recreates Broadway's most pivotal and influential musical, which in turn gives a picture of life in turn-of-the-century Oklahoma. Ironically, the stage show's amazing success hampered the film because classics tend to lose something when transmuted.

Oklahoma!-the-show must be taken in context. In 1943, it was daring and innovative, though today it may seem old hat and traditional. Before *Oklahoma!*, the story musical was little more than an excuse for a few jokes and songs. In *Oklahoma!*, Rodgers and Hammerstein changed things drastically by making a musical which was not a comedy, and which had a strong story *and* songs that either defined the characters or advanced the plot. In addition, where most Broadway musicals have urban settings, *Oklahoma!* is about a rural world in which Kansas City excites imaginations because of its telephones and seven-story buildings.

Oklahoma! portrays a rough-and-tumble time and place. The major conflict is between the farmers and the cowboys, as demonstrated by Aunt Ellen's rousing square dance rendition of "The Farmer and the Cowman," which interrupts a free-for-all. The rivalry between Judd (Rod Steiger) the hired hand, and Curley (Gordon MacRae) the cowboy, for Laurey's (Shirley Jones) affection also emphasizes the intense social conflict. A humorous sub-plot about Ado Annie (who "Cain't Say No") and the infamous "peddler man" (Eddie Albert) helps keep the film light and entertaining.

The best moments in the film are those which give a taste of life in the old West. The opening number shows endless fields of cornstalks which Curley tells us are "as high as an elephant's eye" in the song "Oh What a Beautiful Morning." "Everything's Up-to-Date in Kansas City" describes the marvels of this "modern" town, complete with ragtime dances. The best dance number is the ballet "Out of My Dreams." It is structured and designed like a dream, with rapid shifts of locale and scenery which only make dream sense. At the emotional climax of the dance, Laurey realizes that she loves Curley and not Judd; it is the turning point in the film.

The collected cast and crew of Oklahoma! *under the expansive skies of that celebrated state.*

The film *is* good, but little could have equalled the success of a play which became legendary immediately after it opened, and ran for over 2,000 performances on Broadway.

HELLO, DOLLY! (1969) represents the pinnacle of the big, brassy and empty-headed Broadway musical with nothing on its mind except fun. Based on Thornton Wilder's play, "The Matchmaker," the story concerns Dolly Levi, an effusive busybody whose efforts to wed others eventually work on herself. *Hello, Dolly!* features a spectacular Barbra Streisand performance; the rest of the cast includes Walter Matthau, Tommy Tune, and Tommy Steele. They are all engaging, but are wasted in his routine story which provides some laughs, some plot contrivances, and an excuse for elaborate sets that lavishly recreate turn-of-the-century America.

The key musicial number occurs in a posh Manhattan restaurant. When Dolly arrives the waiters suddenly begin to dance; rows of busboys wheel carts in time to the music, and dancing waiters strut, holding huge platters high in the air. It is truly spectacular and just the sort of dance director Gene Kelly is famous for: humorous, athletic and brilliant. His exciting ensemble dances keep this film from degenerating into fluff. The best solo in the film belongs to Louis Armstrong, who sings Jerry Herman's hit song "Hello, Dolly!"

The real problem with *Hello, Dolly!* was its huge budget. When the film lost millions at the box office, it marked the beginning of the end for movie musicals. Studios saw the failure of this picture as a wholesale rejection of musicals by the public (a case of throwing the baby out with the bathwater). Now that controversy about the film's budget has faded, it can be enjoyed for what it is—a frothy, fancy, empty-headed movie.

MOTHER WORE TIGHTS (1947) presents a romantic view of vaudeville entertainers that quaintly recreates the era between 1900 and 1918.

The story, based on Miriam Young's autobiographical account of her life in vaudeville, centers on a song-and-dance team who marry, achieve fame, and then must face the problems of parenthood. The plot simply provides a series of gentle episodes, vignettes to frame the musical numbers.

The vignettes, however, are solidy threaded with charm. Betty Grable's best performance projects warmth in abundance; her singing and dancing are at their peak. Dan Dailey makes the first of four co-starring appearances opposite her. Although contemporary critics may have been a bit too effusive, proclaiming Grable and Dailey the equal of Astaire and Rogers, their rapport is the film's brightest ingredient. Daughters Mona Freeman and Connie Marshall are also instrumental in making this the biggest box-office hit of Grable's career.

The score is one delight after another. Favorites such as "Kokomo, Indiana," "Swingin' Down the Lane," "Ta Ra Ra Boom De Ay," "Put Your Arms Around Me, Honey," and the Oscar-nominated "You Do" are performed with relish by the two principals. *Mother Wore Tights* breaks no new ground, but every frame of it is lively, buoyant fun.

Barbra Streisand is enthralling in Hello, Dolly!, *but has to compete with a little too much scenery for attention. When she gains center stage, the film is electric.*

Doris Day and her fellow garment workers turn the assembly line into a chorus line in *The Pajama Game.*

THE PAJAMA GAME (1957) is about assembly-line workers in a pajama factory—an unglamorous subject, but one which demonstrates that material for a good musical can be found anywhere. The struggle between management and labor is shown as something akin to a love story. The oddball analogy is embodied in the film's romantic leads. When John Raitt asks Doris Day for a date, she replies, "It wouldn't work; you're a supervisor and I'm the labor committee." But the labor issues are eventually resolved, and the supervisor and the labor committee fall in love.

The musical numbers, written by Richard Adler and Jerry Ross, are the key to *The Pajama Game's* success. They elevate mundane incidents to epic proportions. The drudgery of assembly-line production is converted into the high-spirited number "Racing with the Clock," in which workers at their machines gossip and complain about how fast they have to work. In "Hey There," John Raitt sings a love song into a dictaphone, plays it back, and harmonizes with himself. "Hernando's Hideaway" is a production number centered around the most romantic, illicit place in town, where "all you see are silhouettes." The singers' faces are illuminated by candles that snap on and off in time to the music.

The cast of *The Pajama Game* is another reason for its success. Except for Doris Day they are almost all holdovers from the Broadway show. Day plays a gutsy, sexy, no-nonsense union leader, a far cry from her usual role of an innocent—a stereotype that once prompted Oscar Levant to quip "I knew Doris Day before she became a virgin." The other performers reflect the common man thrust of the play. All the actors mix the ordinary and the extraordinary, keeping their roles from becoming dull and commonplace.

THE MUSIC MAN (1962) was transferred from Broadway almost intact, as one of the best movie adaptations ever. The film presents a picture of life in the Midwest in 1912. The script by Meredith Wilson observes those times with a mix of wry detachment and nostalgia.

The story is of traveling salesman and con-artist Professor Harold Hill (Robert Preston), who travels around the country selling brass band instruments to people in small towns and then leaves before they realize that he can't teach them to play their instruments. However, in River City, Hill makes a fatal mistake: he falls in love with Marian (Shirley Jones), the local librarian. He reforms, and all ends happily.

The musical numbers are perfectly tailored for each character. Hill's songs go from the over-inflated "Seventy-Six Trombones," in which he extols the glories of the greatest band in the world, to the rhythmic salesman's pitch "Trouble," in which he inveigles against the dangers of a pool hall corrupting the morals of River City youth. Marian sings the more romantic "Till There Was You," and the delightful music lesson number in which, to the tune of a piano exercise, her mother explains that none of the women in town will pay attention to Marian even if she is smarter than they are, because they've all got husbands. A very young Ron Howard even gets a solo song—"Gary, Indiana."

Preston is perfect as Hill, projecting charm and sleaze simultaneously. His conversion through love is beautifully handled. Buddy Hackett, as his assistant, gets a rare chance to sing and does it fairly well, and Shirley Jones adds spunk to what could have been a boring role.

All the elements clicked for this film. Even though the film sets are almost identical to those of the stage show, the film does not seem stagey. Morton Da Costa directs with a sure hand and keeps the film at a brisk place. The result is one of the most thoroughly entertaining musicals ever made.

Robert Preston's flawless performance as Professor Harold Hill in The Music Man *came from his having played the role in 883 continuous performances on Broadway.*

THE BEST LITTLE WHORE-HOUSE IN TEXAS (1982), Universal's $26-million movie version of the Broadway hit, benefits from the freedom of its expansive Americana framework.

The plot is based on a true incident—the closing down of a bordello in Texas known as the Chicken Ranch. But the whores are as fresh-faced as Dallas Cowboys cheerleaders, and the opening number, "There's nothin' dirty goin' on," is an accurate comment on all that follows.

Dolly Parton is cast as Miss Mona, a madam with a heart as big as her cleavage. Even her affair with the local sheriff (Burt Reynolds) is innocent and playful. But nasty, self-serving TV crusader Dom De Luise decides to further his career by exposing the immoral goings-on at the ranch.

The contrast between Parton's shining virtue and De Luise's opportunistic "morality" provides ironic humor. Parton is a camera natural, displaying the same tongue-in-cheek charm she did in *Nine to Five*. De Luise's caricature of a public-minded citizen is hilarious.

Leading man Burt Reynolds is the unexpected problem. His acting is a lifeless parody of all his former good-old-boy roles, and his singing ability is non-existent. Frequently, Reynolds' inadequacies are compensated for by Charles Durning. Durning explodes on the screen as a crooked politician. Durning (whose early training for a musical role began when he taught dance at Fred Astaire studios) struts his stuff with comic electricity, fully justifying his 1982 Oscar nomination.

Carol Hall's "Hard Candy Christmas" (top-smash for Parton) is a highlight. So is "I Will Always Love You," which Parton wrote, and which also became a country hit.

The script is thin and the dialogue generally coy, but a good-natured vitality sweeps the action along and makes *The Best Little Whorehouse in Texas* an enjoyable place to visit.

Musicals are known as the vehicles of fantasy. One never expects to find accurate depictions of social situations within their framework. It is therefore ironic that a musical, **WEST SIDE STORY** (1961), should be the most incisive look at teenage gangs that any film has created.

This tale of star-crossed lovers from rival gangs set in a New York slum is important for many reasons. It introduced novel ways of using dance to tell a story. It successfully fused a modern jazz sound with traditional story-related lyrics (very street-smart lyrics at that). It used real locations to connect the story with the real world, and yet it used those locations as precisely controlled as the most constructed studio set. And the Romeo and Juliet angle performs the neat trick of giving this extremely topical tale an element of the universal. *West Side Story* shows that the musical is capable of telling any sort of story.

The striking opening scene sets the standard for the rest of the film. The Jets (the white gang) lurk around the playground, snapping fingers in rhythm to Leonard Bernstein's jazzy score. They are a tough, savage group of punks, yet even while walking down the street they break into dance. Gradually their dancing gets more and more involved with pirouettes and running jumps, and finally they break out into a free and exhilarating high-stepping dance that conveys the message that they own the world. The simple act of vaulting a school fence becomes beautiful when it is choreographed by Jerome Robbins. The scene develops into an outdoor ballet centered around confrontations between the Jets and the rival Sharks (the Puerto Rican gang), which culminates in a beautifully choreographed brawl in the playground. The stylized violence is effective without repelling the audience.

The film's only flaw is the obligatory love interest between the dull Tony (Richard Beymer) and the not-very-Puerto Rican-looking Maria (Natalie Wood). All of the violent kids have more character, are better drawn and have better songs. George Chakiris won an Academy Award for his supporting role as leader of the Sharks, and Rita Moreno won one for her spitfire performance as his girlfriend.

Although *West Side Story* set the stage for more serious Broadway musicals, it had relatively little impact on movies. While audiences may have been ready for more grown up musicals, producers were still wary and there were no follow-up films to this flawed, but fascinating musical.

Sharks' gang leader George Chakiris (left) faces off against several rival Jets. Choreographer Jerome Robbins staged the gang-fighting with such precision that it was indistinguishable from the dancing.

John Travolta is a performer of such magnetic presence that he turned both Saturday Night Fever *(pictured below) and* Grease into huge box-office hits despite the fact that both his roles featured unsympathetic characters.

SATURDAY NIGHT FEVER (1977) captures that glittering instant when disco music and disco dancing were the rage of the nation. That moment was only a short time ago, yet it already seems like history. Nothing dates faster than a dead fad. *Saturday Night Fever* already functions as nostalgia.

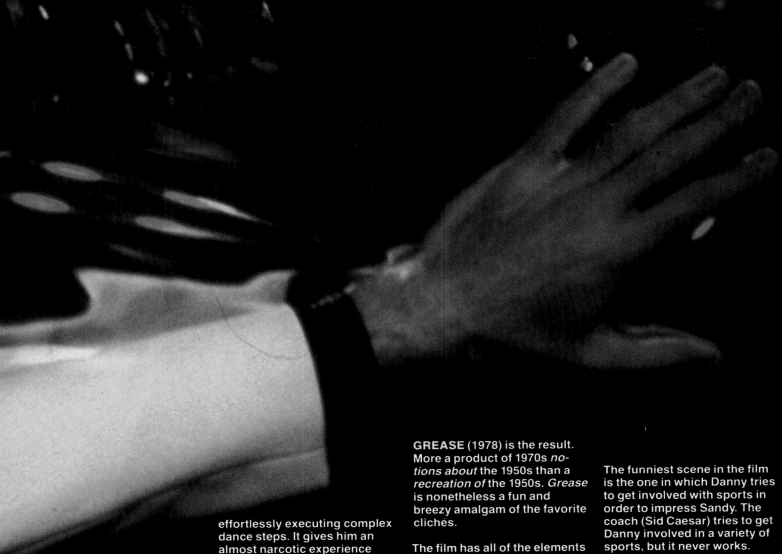

Like so many good films, *Saturday Night Fever* survives because of its originality. The film did not merely recreate the disco phenomenon—it was instrumental in the movement's success. *Saturday Night Fever* helped spread disco dancing to its greatest heights and provided many of the most popular dance moves. The soundtrack album by the Bee Gees was itself the most popular disco music of all.

The film focuses in on the young disco enthusiast Tony Manero (John Travolta). Tony is a working-class Italian in an ethnic neighborhood. He hangs out with his buddies and dances at the discotheque on weekends. His remarkable dancing ability provides his only relief from his humdrum job and family life. On the dance floor he is transformed, effortlessly executing complex dance steps. It gives him an almost narcotic experience that the rest of his life can't match. Tony's dance floor ambitions eventually spark his personal life, and he decides to move out of his dead-end world.

Saturday Night Fever is not a musical in the usual sense: none of its principal characters sing any of the music; they simply dance to pre-recorded music in realistic situations. But the film accurately captures the discotheque experience, wherein the participant is transformed through the dancing and the flashing lights into a fantasy world.

In the 1940s, musicals were churning out romanticized views of the vaudeville era; in the 1950s, *Singin' in the Rain* mythologized the coming of the sound film. By the 1970s, the movies were ready to do a glossy-eyed nostalgia re-write of the Fabulous Fifties:

GREASE (1978) is the result. More a product of 1970s *notions about* the 1950s than a *recreation of* the 1950s, *Grease* is nonetheless a fun and breezy amalgam of the favorite clichés.

The film has all of the elements associated with life in the 1950s—Danny (John Travolta), the tough, cool biker; Sandy (Olivia Newton-John), the goody-two-shoes who doesn't drink, smoke, or have sex; and Rizzo (Stockard Channing), the bad girl who sleeps around. In addition to the stereotypical characters, *Grease* takes place in all of the classic situations: the sock-hop, drive-in, soda-shop, gym, hall lockers, and athletic field.

The best moments of the film do capture the *spirit* of the 1950s. "Summer Nights" has Danny and Sandy each singing their version of their summer romance. Macho Danny tells his friends "We made out under the dock," while good-girl Sandy sings, "We stayed out 'til ten o'clock." To add to the contrast, Sandy innocently skips over picnic tables while Danny illustrates his remarks with lewd body motions.

The funniest scene in the film is the one in which Danny tries to get involved with sports in order to impress Sandy. The coach (Sid Caesar) tries to get Danny involved in a variety of sports, but it never works.

For a musical set in the 1950s, the score is surprisingly contemporary, and that is one of the film's problems. The title song by Barry Gibb, although it may have sold a lot of soundtrack records, immediately destroys the period feeling of the film. Olivia Newton-John, although a fine performer, sings in a contemporary style and is out of place. And much of the dancing in the film is more disco than early rock 'n' roll. Thus, the film really tells more about the 1970s than the 1950s.

Although *Grease* does not succeed as a 1950s parody or a 1950s celebration, it is often amusing and entertaining. The film's greatest achievement, though, was its box-office draw. *Grease* became not only the most successful film of 1978, but the most successful musical ever.

THE BEST OF FAIRY TALES

THE WIZARD OF OZ (1939)
PINOCCHIO (1940)
THE GAY DIVORCEE (1934)
THE LOVE PARADE (1929)
LOVE ME TONIGHT (1932)
YOLANDA AND THE THIEF (1945)
THE PIRATE (1948)
THE ZIEGFIELD FOLLIES (1946)
CAMELOT (1967)
BRIGADOON (1954)
THE WIZ (1978)
POPEYE (1980)
CURLY TOP (1935)
THE 5,000 FINGERS OF DR. T. (1953)
THE MUPPET MOVIE (1979)
MARY POPPINS (1964)

"If your heart is in your dreams, no request is too extreme."

"When You Wish Upon a Star"
Ned Washington and Leigh Harline

Dorothy (Judy Garland), the Scarecrow (Ray Bolger), and the Tin Woodsman (Jack Haley) are "off to see the Wizard, the wonderful Wizard of Oz." The Wizard of Oz truly is a wonderful wiz, the greatest fairy tale ever put to film, musical or otherwise.

The Wicked Witch of the West
(Margaret Hamilton).

To call **THE WIZARD OF OZ** (1939) a classic is missing the point. It is mythic. It is a part of childhood, a part of our culture. Unlike many childhood favorites, however, *The Wizard of Oz* holds up well to adult viewing. It was not made with only children in mind.

It's safe to assume that everyone knows the story of the little girl whisked from Kansas to the fairy land of Oz, only to discover many facts of life: that paradise can have nasty surprises, that changes come from within, and that there's no place like home.

The difficulties behind the making of *The Wizard of Oz* are legendary. About a dozen writers, including Ogden Nash and Herman Mankiewicz, took a shot at writing the script. Several directors actually filmed portions of the movie:

Richard Thorpe, George Cukor (who left after three days to work on *Gone With the Wind*), Victor Fleming, and finally King Vidor, who finished the movie and shot the Kansas scenes.

The casting of the film also has a long and tumultuous history. Producer Arthur Freed wanted a film for his new child sensation, Judy Garland. Although the picture was started with Judy Garland in mind for Dorothy, some people wanted Shirley Temple. And they fought. W. C. Fields was the studio's choice for either Professor Marvel or the Cowardly Lion, depending on whose story you believe. They didn't get him. Jack Haley was cast as the Scarecrow, and Buddy Ebsen—who was a song-and-dance man in the days before Jed Clampett and Barnaby Jones—was cast as the Tin Woodsman. Soon after shooting started, Ebsen had an adverse reaction to the silver paint in his costume and was hospitalized. Haley became the Woodsman, Ray Bolger was brought in as the Scarecrow, and Burt Lahr ended up playing the Cowardly Lion.

The final fight was fought after the film was finished. It concerned the beloved song "Over the Rainbow." Top studio men thought it slowed down the picture and wanted it cut, but Arthur Freed was adamant about it remaining in—and of course it went on to win an Oscar.

The film is filled with magical moments. In one of the most brilliant moments in the film Dorothy opens the door to her house and sees the Technicolor world of Oz. Although the transition from black and white to color may seem creatively inspired, it was a decision born out of necessity. There was a limit to the amount of time they could use the Technicolor camera. Though her total time on screen is less than ten minutes, all of Margaret Hamilton's scenes as the witch are perfect. She dominates the film. Her death is another high point. And of course, the first and second visits to the Wizard are spellbinders: the first when Dorothy and Company are overwhelmed by his power, and the second when he is revealed as a fraud.

The songs are magical. Harold Arlen, who wrote the music, has never been in finer form, and lyricist E. Y. Harburg indulges in his delightful penchant for playing with words. "Which old witch" and "But I could show my prowess, be a lion not a meow-ess," are examples of Harburg at his most playful.

One reason the film remains so solidly in the mind is that it's so frightening. Modern children's books may be stripped of their frightening elements, but children have delighted in terror since the days of the Brothers Grimm. Who can forget the Wicked Witch's invasion of the idyllic Munchkinland, or the evil talking trees, or the menacing flying monkees who tear the Scarecrow apart?

When *The Wizard of Oz* is broadcast on television it is missing four minutes, which have been trimmed for commercials. The cuts include some shots of Munchkinland and the opening title, which dedicates the film to "the Young at Heart." One interesting thing to watch for is the first scene with the Cowardly Lion. As Bert Lahr says, "Is my nose bleedin'?" Judy Garland has to stifle a laugh. She regains her composure quickly enough. Another thing to watch for is the Wizard's balloon; it bears the inscription, "State Fair, Omaha."

Perhaps the final irony about *The Wizard of Oz* is that though the film has been universally recognized as a classic—and though it may be the most widely seen film ever—it was pretty much a flop on its initial release, barely making back its production costs. It was only because of television screenings, which started in 1956, that the film became universally known. It is worthy of its fame.

Dorothy and her pals deep in the Magic Forest, an example of Hollywood studio artistry at its best. The entire film—including the scenes in Kansas—were shot indoors on a sound stage.

Gepetto puts the finishing touches on his prize puppet, Pinocchio. He finds that what is an excellent puppet can be a very bad little boy.

The animated features of Walt Disney usually include a few songs, but PINOCCHIO (1940) is so successful with its songs (and accompanying dance numbers) that it is actually a great musical. There are heartfelt and memorable ballads (such as Jiminy Cricket singing "When You Wish Upon a Star," which rivals Bing Crosby for gentle soulfulness), rollicking production numbers (such as the bad boys entering and enjoying Pleasure Isle), and great dance numbers (such as Pinocchio's dance of joy when he discovers that he can move without strings).

Pinocchio is based on a book by Collodi about a lonely puppet maker named Gepetto who wants a son. Because Gepetto is a good man, the blue fairy grants his wish and gives one of his puppets the gift of life. However, Pinocchio is not immediately a real boy; he cannot be one until he shows such human characteristics as compassion and selflessness. Pinocchio actually acts more like a real boy than one might like to believe, and these fail-

The film also has several classic tunes by Leigh Harline and Ned Washington: "I've Got No Strings," "Hi Diddle Dee Dee (An Actor's Life for Me)," "Give a Little Whistle," and "When You Wish Upon a Star" (beautifully sung by Cliff "Ukulele Ike" Edwards, this tune eventually became the Disney theme song).

ings get him into a series of difficulties. The allure of stage success traps him in a stage show with marionettes run by the evil Stromboli; the wish to play and eat candy all day lures him to Pleasure Isle where children are turned into donkeys; and his thoughtlessness causes Gepetto to roam the world in search of his son, only to be trapped inside Monstro the whale. Throughout these adventures, Pinocchio is accompanied by his "conscience," Jiminy Cricket.

In terms of the animation, there has never been a more complex film. The craftsmanship that went into the film is evident in every meticulously drawn frame. The opening shot alone is worth the price of admission. It is a bird's eye view of Gepetto's village. The camera swoops down, shifting perspective, going in among the houses and finally landing in Gepetto's room. Usually animation is done with characters against a steady flat background, but for *Pinocchio* the background had to be redrawn with each camera shift, and the opening sequence cost a staggering $200,000 in 1940 dollars! Today, when speed is the important word, cartoons are rarely this lush.

THE GAY DIVORCEE (1934) created the "myth" of Fred Astaire and Ginger Rogers. Fred and Ginger as romantic ideals lead lives of extreme splendor. Their magnificent style and breezy ballroom manner create the fairy tale of ultimate love among the rich and urbane.

Fred and Ginger dance "The Continental" in an elaborate 17-minute production number. It went on to become the first song to win an Academy Award.

The story is set in the world of the ultra-rich. Ginger Rogers wants to get a divorce from her husband and needs a co-respondent to spend the night with her. Through a mix-up, she thinks Astaire is the gigolo. This mistaken identity is the major plot complication. This type of story was used, with variations, in all their films and provides the framework for the Astaire-Rogers formula.

One scene common to most of their films is "the meeting," the scene where Astaire first sets eyes on Ginger Rogers. In *The Gay Divorcee*, Rogers gets her dress caught in a trunk at a customs station. She calls for help and Astaire comes to her aid. His efforts rip her dress and she leaves in a huff.

Astaire and Rogers end up at the same seaside resort. Astaire is smitten and, impulsive boy that he is, proposes to her. Though slightly charmed by his impertinence, Rogers rejects him. The stage is now set for "the seduction"—usually the key element in their films. Alone with Rogers in a room, Astaire breaks into "Night and Day." During the second chorus, Rogers tries to flee. In time to the music, he runs ahead and cuts her off, then catapults the scene into a dance by doing a few graceful twirls. He grabs her, does several steps by himself, and pulls her towards him. She responds by spinning into his arms. They start to dance together. Rogers smiles with a warm glow, succumbing to Astaire's feet; then she regains her composure and tries to leave. Astaire seizes her arm, she slaps him, and he recoils in dance, gracefully losing his balance, reeling around and around, his tails flying. He pursues her, and this time she is conquered. They hold each other tightly and finally he deposits her, totally drained, into a chair. Astaire has made love to Rogers through dance, an allusion made clear by Astaire's offer of a cigarette to the fulfilled Rogers. The amazing thing about this number is that it is simplicity itself. There are no gimmicks, no fake sets, no trick photography; it is only Fred Astaire dancing with Ginger Rogers in total harmony.

The Gay Divorcee's big production number is "The Continental," which became the first song to win an Academy Award. The dramatic set is stark black and white, from the shiny reflecting floor to the dancers' clothing. Astaire and Rogers do a chorus of the dance, and then hordes of dancers do variations on it. While some of these are interesting—revolving doors with chorus girls in each compartment, for instance —it is Astaire and Rogers who ultimately hold center stage.

During the Depression, movie audiences loved to see stories about the rich and privileged. The films dealt with love en-

tanglements in lieu of economic strife. One of the most popular tactics in early musicals was to create a mythical modern kingdom with a lonely and beautiful princess; then some handsome commoner or loveable rogue would come along to rescue her from her

Jeanette MacDonald had quite a sexy presence in her early films, before the Hayes Code cracked down on film morality.

pampered misery. **THE LOVE PARADE** (1929) and **LOVE ME TONIGHT** (1932) are the two finest examples of this type of musical. Much of their tone and style, as well as the slight plot complications, came from popular operettas such as *The Merry Widow.*

Both *The Love Parade* and *Love Me Tonight* feature Jeanette MacDonald and Maurice Chevalier. Jeanette MacDonald came to films directly from operettas and was ideally suited for her roles. In addition to her singing voice, she had an innocent look combined with a covertly sexual manner that was perfect for these innuendo-laden films. Maurice Chevalier, a cabaret-style singer with an irreverent and jovial manner, came to epitomize the Parisian for American audiences. In his films there is always only one thing on his mind: the conquest of love.

The Love Parade features Chevalier as the Sylvanian ambassador to Paris. However, Chevalier is soon run out of town for having seduced nearly every woman within the city. As he departs, he sings "Paris, Stay the Same," while the Parisian women wave goodbye. Back in Sylvania he is re-

dressed by the Queen (MacDonald), who just can't seem to take her eyes off him. As the Queen is in need of a husband, Chevalier finds a use for his talents. The marriage, however, is unhappy. MacDonald, as Queen, is in charge, and Chevalier finds he is useless except in bed. There are a number of funny (if obvious) jokes about sexual roles, and the film's rather feminist stance seems pretty savvy.

The Love Parade was made by Ernst Lubitsch, an extremely talented director who specialized in light sex comedies. He had a natural camera instinct that made his films flow effortlessly through their paces. He knew how to coax the best performances out of his actors, and used subtle details to connect the story. *The Love Parade* is an important musical because it invented many of the principles that later became standard practice. Lubitsch made the musical numbers flow from the plot and staged them with movement and imagination. His wry touches, such as having a dog sing a chorus of one of Chevalier's boastful songs, insured that the film would never drip sentiment like many operettas.

Love Me Tonight features Chevalier as a Parisian tailor. His status as a commoner allows him to ridicule and debunk royalty even as he is wooing and winning Princess Jeanette. The film is every bit as witty and pithy as *The Love Parade,* but it has an even greater fluid-

ity of style and camera movement. The songs by Richard Rodgers and Lorenz Hart are so completely woven into the script that it is often hard to tell where they begin and end. There are rhymed dialogue passages that are actually dramatic scenes set to music.

The staging of the musical numbers by director Rouben Mamoulian is also quite innovative. He uses music to link disparate scenes together. The grand sweeping camera movements are synchronized to the soundtrack, so that the entire film seems like a waltz. *Love Me Tonight* is a remarkable achievement.

The fantasy world of mythical kingdoms and lonely royalty recurs in **YOLANDA AND THE THIEF** (1945) with a twist: the mythical kingdom is the realistic half of the film. The film contains dream sequences within its fairy tale plot that carry it into the most extreme flights of imagination. This film is also a favorite among dance aficionados for its very appropriate use of ballet dance.

The imagination at work in *Yolanda and the Thief* is Vincente Minnelli's; the director's keen sense of color and knowledge of stage design allowed him to create dream worlds on top of dream worlds. Fred Astaire and Frank Morgan play a couple of con men trying to bilk heiress Lucille Bremer. Bremer mistakes Astaire for her guardian angel, and Astaire gladly uses that pretext to get within arm's reach of her jewels. Unfortunately for his criminal instincts, he falls in love with her. Only then is the true guardian angel revealed.

While Astaire is trying to decide whether to be a lover or a crook, he has some interesting dreams. In one he dances with Bremer on a floor that slopes gently to infinity. In other dreams he is chased by some of the most Dali-esque images ever filmed. The finest achievement of *Yolanda and the Thief* is its ability to match set design and decor with the sound and mood of the music.

Fred Astaire and Lucille Bremer dance in Fred's mind while he tries to choose between love and money. Fred's dreams are as lovely as his dancing and Yolanda and the Thief contains several of them, some of the most visually imaginative work that director Vincente Minnelli has ever done.

THE PIRATE (1948) posits that fantasy is more believable than reality because it is more enjoyable. This concept becomes the springboard for a high-spirited, dynamic, funny, and intelligent musical.

The fantasy vs. reality theme is tightly woven into the story. Judy Garland's fantasy is to be swept off her feet by the most evil pirate of them all, Mack the Black. The fantasy of both Walter Slezak and Gene Kelly is to sweep Judy Garland off her feet, but she dislikes the fat and dull Slezak, and is put off by Kelly, the uncivilized actor. Since actors deal in illusions, it isn't too much trouble for Kelly to assume the role of Mack the Black and come for Garland. The irony is that Slezak is really Mack the Black, although he seems more like a bookkeeper.

The musical high points of the film are connected with the fantasy theme. Under hypnosis Garland discloses her infatuation with the Black Pirate and belts out "Mack the Black" explaining "Ladies go to pieces over pieces of eight." Later, when Kelly is impersonating the pirate, she fantasizes about his life on the sea. Dressed like Douglas Fairbanks, with a ragged shirt over his muscular thighs and a bandana around his head, Kelly and his pirates pillage a ship as frenzied music plays. Kelly climbs the ship's mast to cut its sails, dramatically throws down his torch (thereby creating a huge orange fireball that lights up the sky), and finally slides down on a rope, knife clenched in his teeth. No wonder Garland is in love with this romanticized picture of a pirate.

The film works because it is perfectly cast. As in *The Wizard of Oz*, Garland plays a dreamer (a point brought home at one point when she cries "Aunt Inez, Aunt Inez, I want to go home!"). Garland's gift for comedy is also displayed to its best advantage. After Kelly has taken over the town and demanded one night with Garland, another girl offers to go in her place. Garland delivers a perfectly timed, huffy, "He asked for *me!*" Gene Kelly's role is also perfect for him. He gets to do many spectacular dances, as well as to indulge in his penchant for overacting. All of the performers seem to be enjoying themselves and that, more than anything else, is the secret to the success of *The Pirate.*

THE ZIEGFIELD FOLLIES (1946) starts in heaven, where each person has a private cloud and bath. Florenz Ziegfield has a particularly opulent cloud, with scenes from all his shows floating on the wall. Something is missing from Ziegfield's afterlife, however. He wants to put on one more spectacular extravaganza. He gets his wish, and the result is a spectacular, hallucinogenic, musical revue. A cavalcade of stars, it includes Fred Astaire, Lucille Ball, Esther Williams, Gene Kelly, Lucille Bremer, and Judy Garland.

The quality of their skits is uneven. The high point of the film is "The Babbit and the Bromide," a Fred Astaire and Gene Kelly duet. It is a fascinating and unique opportunity to see the different styles of these two great dancers together. Even though they match each other step for step, they're not trying to be alike. Astaire is more graceful. At the same time, Kelly dances more athletically and boisterously than Astaire does. The dance is filled with horseplay. Kelly and Astaire also waltz together, and they make terrific partners. But the screen was not big enough for these two superstars, and they had to wait 30 years before being reunited in *That's Entertainment, Part II.*

Vincente Minnelli, who directed most of *The Ziegfield Follies*, obviously tried to do something different and important with this film. The fact that he misses as often as he succeeds should not be held against him.

Anyone who has ever dreamed of utopia will recognize their heart's desire in **CAMELOT** (1967). The tale of King Arthur's great society and the great love affair that ended it is told in beautiful ballads that evoke a medieval feeling. The traditional musical elements—like fantasy sets and dance numbers—are downplayed to concentrate on the story.

Spurred by the teachings of his mentor Merlin, King Arthur strives to create a perfect society, with reason and law as its cornerstone. He forms a body of knights, known as the Knights of the Round Table, who fight for truth and justice. Sir Lancelot, the purest of the pure, comes to join them and becomes Arthur's best friend. He also falls in love with Arthur's wife, Lady Guinevere.

They have an affair, and Arthur has to choose between being thought a cuckold and sentencing them to death. Finally they are caught in the act, and Arthur has no choice. His wife is tied to a stake, about to be burned, when Lancelot comes to the rescue. After the bloodshed, the people want revenge, and Arthur sees his society crumble with bloodlust and a series of wars.

Camelot is an especially poetic film. It is not surprising its music was written by Lerner and Loewe, the same team that wrote *Brigadoon*, another musical about a magic land.

When the film came out, Richard Harris and Vanessa Redgrave were compared unfavorably to Richard Burton and Julie Andrews, who had played Arthur and Guinevere on Broadway. But Harris and Redgrave are actually very good, each making the most of the tender sequences, and playing off each other nicely.

Camelot represents the end to many things. The film concerns an end of innocence and the end of a magical era. The show was John F. Kennedy's favorite musical and became associated with the Kennedy Administration, which also ended tragically. But most importantly it ended the collaboration between Frederic Loewe and Alan Jay Lerner.

The round table in Camelot.

The Ziegfield Follies *doesn't allow a dreary plot to drag down its musical sequences. because there isn't any plot! It's a hit-or-miss affair with plenty of hits. Rarely seen, this film holds lots of surprises. Here, Fred Astaire does a Latin dance on top of bongo drums.*

BRIGADOON (1954) is like an extended dream. It sets a warm love story in a magical land. The talent that went into making the film is also like a dream: Vincente Minnelli directed Gene Kelly and Cyd Charisse in a Lerner and Loewe musical.

Brigadoon is the story of a town in the Scottish highlands that exists only one day every hundred years. Two days after this miracle occurs (Brigadoon Time), Gene Kelly and Van Johnson, vacationing Americans, stumble across the town. They accept the 18th-century ways as local custom. Then Kelly meets one of the residents, Cyd Charisse, and falls in love. Once the town's secret is revealed to him, Kelly must choose between living in the modern world or staying in Brigadoon with Charisse.

Brigadoon was Lerner and Loewe's first Broadway success, with many lilting and beautiful melodies. These songs are fully realized in the film. Gene Kelly sings the hit of the show, "Almost Like Being In Love," then does a carefree dance down a garden path, ending with a soft shoe in the dirt near some farm animals. The setting for the duet "The Heather on the Hill" is lush and romantic, with Kelly and Charisse standing in the middle of a golden field, a tranquil lake and mountains looming in the background. By the end of the film, the viewer is as much in love with Brigadoon as Kelly is.

Brigadoon.

THE WIZ (1978) is a retelling of *The Wizard of Oz* with an all-black cast. *The Wiz* takes on a social dimension even as it revels in fantasy.

The film's social message is brought out through its deviance from the traditional story. Instead of being a Kansas girl, Dorothy (Diana Ross) is a 24-year-old woman who lives in Harlem. Oz is New York City south of 125th Street, a demarcation which implies that the mid-town and financial districts of Manhattan are as far removed from everyday life in Harlem as Oz is from Kansas. The Scarecrow (Michael Jackson) is found in a vacant lot near a burnt-out tenement. The deadly poppy field is changed into an opium and sex den. Whenever Dorothy encounters a yellow-brick-road taxi it flashes an off-duty sign and drives away, and when the foursome make it to the Emerald City Doorway, they are asked to use the servants' entrance.

While many of the scenes in the film are delightful, they never quite equal the stunning sets they're being played in front of. The dance numbers are sloppily choreographed and shot in a chaotic fashion with pointless, jarring editing. Still, much of *The Wiz* is excellent thanks to such dynamic cast members as Lena Horne, Diana Ross and Richard Pryor. It is important to note that the problems with *The Wiz* have nothing to do with its concept, which is continually winning and innovative. For all its flaws, *The Wiz* is one of the most imaginative musicals in recent years.

Tony Walton was the set designer for The Wiz *and he did a magician's job of creating the land of Oz out of New York City motifs. Here, the city hall becomes the Wiz's chamber. Seen with Dorothy (Diana Ross) is the Tin Man (Nipsey Russell), the Lion (Ted Ross) and the Scarecrow (Michael Jackson).*

POPEYE (1980) is an attempt to recreate on film the cartoon world of the pipe-smoking, spinach-eating, malapropic cartoon character. *Popeye* cartoons featured a nightmarish world populated with grotesque and fascinating characters who would have felt at home in a Dickens novel.

The ever-mumbling Popeye is played by comedian Robin Williams, who beautifully captures Popeye's speech, charming naiveté, and his "senske of humor." Popeye's girlfriend is the stringy, snippy, fussy Olive Oyl. She is played to perfection by Shelley Duvall. She is a cartoon character embodied in poses that almost seem human. Olive Oyl is uncompromisingly unappealing, so, of course, both Bluto and Popeye fall in love with her. Her character is best seen in little moments: at dinner she asks for a glass, is given one and whines "That's a short fat ugly glass."

The last important character in the film is Wimpy, played by Paul Dooley, the unscrupulous, gluttonous wastrel whose motto is "I'll gladly pay you Tuesday for a hamburger today." Wimpy is never maliciously evil, just self-involved and concerned with his stomach. Wimpy steals the screen whenever he appears.

These characters are set loose in a ramshackle, sprawling town called Sweethaven and go through the motions of a plot. When *Popeye* is on target, it is marvelously cartoonlike. But it flounders in the last half hour, becoming almost incoherent.

►

Popeye (Robin Williams) is strong to the finish cause he "eatsk" his spinach. Shelley Duvall is Olive Oyl.

In 1938, Shirley Temple was the top box-office draw in America, ahead of Clark Gable and Greta Garbo. By 1940, her career was pretty much over. She continued to make films in the 40s, but was not very remarkable as a teenager.

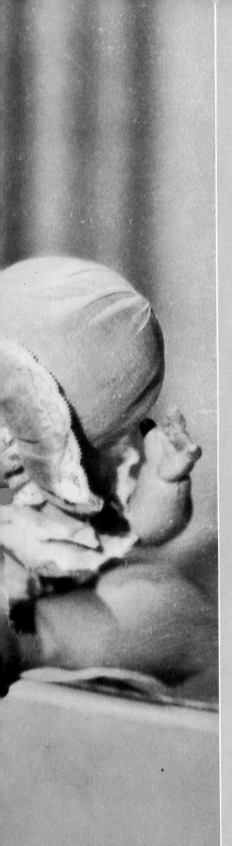

Shirley Temple was the ultimate screen performer. Dancing, singing, acting—she could do it all. Realizing that she wouldn't be a child forever, the studios churned out her films at the rate of three a year. This often resulted in unpolished films, though Temple's performance was almost always superior.

CURLY TOP (1935), one of her best films, has a strong story about an orphan secretly adopted by a wealthy man.

The story begins on a rainy night at the Lake Side Orphanage. All the orphans say their prayers and Shirley adds "take care of my duck and pony." Later Temple eats lunch and sings "Animal Crackers in My Soup," while the other orphans accompany her on tinkling glasses. This spectacle is discovered by the orphanage trustees—who naturally don't like songs and especially don't like Shirley Temple. But one of the trustees, John Boles, takes her under his wing.

For the remainder of the film, Temple does cute things, making observations like "I like to make things to eat and I 'specially like to eat them," and singing cute songs. In "When I Grow Up," Temple tells what she'll do as a woman. She appears as a bride in a wedding outfit and then as an old woman with a cane and granny glasses.

Memorable moments in other Shirley Temple films are the dance up and down the stairs she does with a young Buddy Ebsen in *Captain January,* her rendition of "On the Good Ship Lolly Pop" in *Bright Eyes,* and her "Polly Wolly Doodle" song-and-dance duet with the incomparable Bill "Bojangles" Robinson in *The Little Rebel.*

THE 5,000 FINGERS OF DR. T. (1953) may well be the strangest musical fantasy ever made. It sprang from the fervent imagination of Theodore Geisel, who writes children's books under the name "Dr. Seuss."

Cruel piano teacher Dr. Terwilliker (played with eye-popping glee by Hans Conried) is in the process of opening a camp for 500 piano students. What the parents don't know is that he plans to keep all five hundred of them playing a mile-long piano forever. If this sounds like a piano student's nightmare to you, you're right. One of the doctor's students, little Bart Collins (Tommy Rettig) must try to stop this madman.

The overall look of the film is unique. The sets are done like Dr. Seuss drawings with uneven lines, strange perspectives, and odd combinations of colors. There are many visual jokes, and the musical numbers are strange as well. "Terwilliker Academy," a parody of college songs, proclaims that T.A. is the only poison-ivy-league school. The oddest number takes place in the dungeon-for-people-who-play-instruments-other-than-the-piano. Dr. T. wants to rid the world of screechy piccolos, nauseating trumpets, and other vile instruments. Dr. Seuss has gone wild inventing his own instruments. One musician plays a radiator; another with a long stick on the end of his nose swings from side to side hitting gongs.

The 5,000 Fingers of Dr. T. works well as a children's film. What kid hasn't wanted to kill his piano teacher? What kid hasn't felt that no one was listening to him? What kid hasn't thought his parents were idiots? Adults may find it entertaining, too.

It's hard to find a more accomplished musical of the past few years than **THE MUPPET MOVIE** (1979). Jim Henson's loveable and witty puppet characters not only manage the difficult feat of carrying a nearly plotless feature film for 94 minutes, but they pull off the even more difficult task of incorporating singing and dancing.

The nominal plot has Kermit the Frog traveling cross-country to Hollywood to become a movie star. Along the way he picks up Muppet friends and dodges a fast-food frog-leg entrepreneur. The film features a dual set of cameo appearances. On the one hand, nearly every memorable character from the television show is worked into the film somewhere. On the other hand, Kermit and friends encounter busloads of Hollywood notables in the flesh, including Bob Hope, Richard Pryor, Steve Martin, Orson Welles, and Mel Brooks. The great charm of the Muppets has always been their ability to interact with humans, and Henson exploits this fully. His terrific sense of humor shines throughout. The tone of the film is reminiscent of the old Rocky and Bullwinkle cartoons.

From the opening number, in which Kermit sings and plays banjo from a lily pad in a vast swamp, to the huge closing finale, "The Rainbow Song," Henson demonstrates a remarkable knowledge of precisely how to stage and photograph a musical number. One regrets that he wasn't around for the glory days with Gene Kelly and company.

MARY POPPINS (1964) is the delightfully daffy tale of a very eccentric English nanny. Based on children's stories by P.L. Travers, this Walt Disney film imaginatively presents the adventures of a magical nurse-maid in Edwardian London. The wonders which Disney Studios could achieve are put to their fullest advantage here, lifting (literally) nearly every scene with clever special effects. It also features some of the best combined live action and animation sequences ever created.

Two children, Jane (Karen Dotrice) and Michael (Matthew Garber), are kept isolated and ignored by their wealthy parents. They are never allowed to have fun. They keep wearing out their nannies until the stern and proper Mary Poppins (Julie Andrews) drops in. She teaches them discipline and respect, but she also gives them love and adventure. Her magical powers can sweep them away to all sorts of places. They also meet Mary's menagerie of friends, including Burt the Chimney Sweep (Dick Van Dyke) and Uncle Albert (Ed Wynn), whose giggling keeps him on the ceiling.

In addition to being a wondrous and vivacious fantasy, *Mary Poppins* is a very nice musical, with inventive dances (precision chimney sweep drills on rooftops and soft-shoes with penguins) and great witty songs by Richard M. and Robert B. Sherman. It's hard to forget the lyrics of "Spoonful of Sugar," "Chim-Chim-Cheree," or "Supercali-fragilisticexpialidocious."

Probably the best compliment one can pay a children's film is to say that adults will like it as well. That's certainly true here. The film stays light and whimsical without ever getting too sentimental. Of all the nice things to say about *Mary Poppins*, surely the most noteworthy is the film debut of Julie Andrews. Her performance won her an Academy Award and many hearts.

In her acceptance speech for winning the Academy Award for her role in Mary Poppins, Julie Andrews thanked "Jack Warner for making it all possible." She was referring to his refusal to cast her in the film version of her Broadway triumph, "My Fair Lady," thus freeing her to do the Disney film.

THE BEST OF FARAWAY PLACES

THE KING AND I (1956)
GIGI (1959)
THE SOUND OF MUSIC (1965)
SOUTH PACIFIC (1958)
INTERNATIONAL HOUSE (1933)
THE ROAD TO BALI (1952)
SILK STOCKINGS (1957)
WEEKEND IN HAVANA (1941)
ON A CLEAR DAY YOU CAN SEE FOREVER (1970)
FUNNY FACE (1957)
ON THE TOWN (1949)
AN AMERICAN IN PARIS (1951)
FIDDLER ON THE ROOF (1971)
MY FAIR LADY (1964)
OLIVER! (1968)
TOP HAT (1935)
FLYING DOWN TO RIO (1933)

*"Come with me where moon beams light Tahitian skies,
And starlight waters linger in your eyes."*

"Pagan Love Song"
Arthur Freed and Nacio Herb Brown

*Rossano Brazzi longs for his love, Mitzi Gaynor, in the romantic
tropical atmosphere of South Pacific.*

THE KING AND I (1956) Rodgers and Hammerstein's most complex musical, dealing with the theme of cultural contamination. Hollywood usually prefers light Broadway musicals to heavy ones, so the fact that *The King and I* is entertaining is almost as amazing as the fact that it was successfully filmed.

The King and I is based on *Anna and the King of Siam*, a novel that tells the story of a British schoolteacher brought to Siam to educate the King's children in Western ways. The film revolves around the fascinating King of Siam (Yul Brynner), who is vain and childish, but also understanding. The King is trapped running an old-fashioned country in a modern age, and Anna's teachings only confuse him. In Siam, the King determines what is right—even whether the earth is round or flat. Western thought, however, uses the scientific method to find the truth. The differences between the two methods have very real consequences for the King. For if the King can be wrong, what of his power? The turning point of the story occurs when

the King is about to whip a slave girl, but Anna says he will be a barbarian if he does that. His will crumbles. He spares the girl, and his authority is destroyed forever. The shame kills him, and as he lies on his death bed, he watches the heir apparent further Westernize Siam.

In the film Anna encounters a culture different from her own, one which she feels she must change. She challenges the people by teaching that Siam is not at the center of the universe, that the world is round, and that slavery is bad. This causes doubts for everyone, including the King who sings,

"There are times I almost think I am not sure of what I absolutely know." To further confuse the King, Anna instructs him in Victorian morality: "Sometimes things can't be just a question of what we want, Your Highness, but of what is right." This, however, is no objective fact. Which cul-

King Yul Brynner witnesses centuries of Siamese tradition crumble from his deathbed. Brynner was nominated for an Oscar for his performance, which he originated on Broadway.

ture is right? The film is stacked against the Siamese. Of course beating slaves is inhumane, and of course the world is round, but when the children realize that some of what they have been taught is wrong, it is only natural for them to wonder what else is wrong. When the King is on his

deathbed, his son announces an end to the practice of bowing to the King.

The musical numbers are solid, though not well-integrated into the film. If they were all cut out it would not make much of a difference to the story. On a boat in the har-

bor, Anna tells her son her secret for coping with fear in "I Whistle a Happy Tune." At her first school session Anna gets to know her students through the song "Getting to Know You," and then performs a fan dance with one of her students. The "March of the Siamese Children" number

consists of dozens of cute kids walking into a room and bowing to their father and Anna, all set to Richard Rodgers' lovely tune, which probably had more impact on the stage. An interesting sequence has a Siamese version of "Uncle Tom's Cabin" staged by Jerome Robbins. The various dancers enact the story of a runaway slave, Eliza, as she is pursued by the evil Simon LeGree. The dancers create the scenery and props, and while it is not authentic, it is interesting. The most famous number in the film is "Shall We Dance," in which Anna instructs the King in the art of social dancing, and he gets a bit too close for her comfort.

The King and I succeeds because of stellar performances by Deborah Kerr (with singing dubbed by Marni Nixon) and Yul Brynner. Kerr is the epitomy of the repressed Victorian woman, feisty and critical. With his bald head and angular eyebrows Brynner is superb at creating a member of an alien culture. However, he is not the least bit Oriental, especially when contrasted with the real Orientals with which the film is populated. Perhaps that is why The King and I was banned in Siam when it came out.

This film demonstrates that songs and serious themes can go together, though few film musicals have been as successful in this regard as The King and I.

GIGI (1959) is an opulent, witty, and charming film that captures the special spirit of the MGM musical. It takes place in Paris in the year 1900 and tells the story of a young girl raised to be a courtesan. Maurice Chevalier, who serves as the narrator Honore Lachaille, sets the tone as he introduces himself, "Born? Paris. Date? Not lately. This is 1900, so let's just say not in this century . . . . Profession? Lover . . . . Married? What for." He casts his eye on a playground full of frolicking youngsters that includes a playful, awkward girl—Gigi (Leslie Caron), and sings "Thank Heaven for Little Girls."

Gigi is cared for by her grandmother and great-aunt. Aunt Alicia (Isabel Jeans) gives her lessons in how to be a lady, explaining that "bad table manners have broken up more households than infidelity." The instructions are necessary because Gigi and her family are not "ordinary" people. "Instead of getting married at once," the aunt says, "*we* get married at last."

The other important person in Gigi's life is Gascon Lachaille (Louis Jourdan), an incredibly rich man who takes no joy in his wealth. The only thing that interests him is little Gigi, whom he visits constantly.

During the course of the film, Gigi grows up. When the family realizes that Gascon is in love with her, they embark on an extensive training campaign to turn Gigi into a lady. When Gascon realizes he loves her, he does what any Frenchman would do: he makes her his mistress. The newly-trained Gigi, however, is now like other women: discussing society matters, discoursing on jewelry, dancing perfectly. In short, a bore. But Gascon discovers that his love for Gigi runs deeper than he thought, and he marries her.

Gigi was based on the novel by Colette, with book and score by Alan Jay Lerner and

Louis Jourdan confides in Maurice Chevalier.

Gascon (Louis Jourdan) looks at the suddenly grown-up Gigi (Leslie Caron) with love in his eyes—a typical Frenchman.

Frederic Loewe. It may just be coincidence, but the film bears many similarities to *My Fair Lady*, another Lerner and Loewe musical, in which a woman is educated in breeding and manners so that she may take her place in society and catch a man. The artificial rules of society are lampooned in both pieces.

Another similarity between *My Fair Lady* and *Gigi* is the many spoken songs for which the tune provides only an outline, such as "I Remember It Well," which Chevalier and Hermione Gingold talk through rhythmically, lapsing into the melody occasionally. It is both a meditation on aging *and* a fond love song.

Gigi, of course, is not *My Fair Lady*. It is a much warmer film, chiefly due to its wonderful cast. Leslie Caron is perfect as Gigi, convincingly portraying both the young, immature girl, rushing everywhere, slouching in her chair with a pout, and Gigi the lady. Caron is as beautiful and elegant as any lady who ever lived, yet she still seems sixteen, and that makes her transformation all the more stunning. Louis Jourdan also succeeds with his difficult role as the bored Gascon. Played by a less skilled actor, Gascon could have come out as a heavy; instead he gains sympathy because though he has all the riches he could possibly need, he cannot enjoy life. Isabel Jeans also converts Aunt Alicia into an understandable, though not necessarily likeable character. The surprise of the film, however, is Maurice Chevalier. Continually playing a character who takes life as it comes, he gets the perfect song for his old age, "I'm Glad I'm Not Young Anymore," and convinces the viewer that old age is best.

Gigi was justly rewarded by the Academy Awards with awards for best picture, song, direction, writing, cinematography, and set direction, with an honorary award for Maurice Chevalier.

THE SOUND OF MUSIC (1965) has acquired a reputation as the sugariest musical ever made. However, while there are many cute things in the film, it also confronts genuine evil, which serves as a balance. Taken in part the film can be ridiculed for its wholesome attitude, but as a whole it works.

The opening *is* perhaps too cute. In a convent, nuns gossip about Maria (Julie Andrews), a postulant. Maria is nothing but trouble, getting mud on her robes, enjoying nature, and "always late for everything except for every meal." Maria is assigned to be nanny for Colonel Von Trapp (Christopher Plummer) and his seven children, before she decides whether to become a nun. Since his wife died, Von Trapp has run his house like one of his ships, with a military discipline which leaves no time for play. Maria softens his heart and they fall in love just before the takeover of Von Trapp's beloved Austria by the Nazis.

The two best songs are "Do-Re-Mi," in which Maria teaches the children music by giving a name to each note of the scale, and "Edelweiss," Oscar Hammerstein's last lyric, written as an Austrian folk song that is sung defiantly as the Nazis look on.

The Sound of Music received a very enthusiastic response from general audiences and was one of the top box office attractions for a long time.

Some musicals are so strong and so packed with crowd-pleasing elements that they automatically capture the public. Stars and director are almost irrelevant. Rodgers and Hammerstein's **SOUTH PACIFIC** (1958) is a prime example of a virtually failure-proof property.

The film manages to spotlight every virtue that made the Broadway hit so memorable. Exotic South Sea locales provide a picturesque and romantic escape. The play's dramatic structure owes its strength to James Michener's Pulitzer Prize winning *Tales of the South Pacific*. And the immortal score features such standards as "A Cockeyed Optimist," "There Is Nothin' Like a Dame," "Some Enchanted Evening," and "I'm In Love with a Wonderful Guy."

Mitzi Gaynor is pert and appealing as U.S. Navy nurse Nellie Forbush, who falls in love with French planter Emile de Becque (Rossano Brazzi). Conflict arises when she discovers he has two Eurasian children, offspring of a Polynesian mistress. Her prejudiced rejection of him ties in neatly with the sub-plot involving American Lieutenant Joseph Cable (John Kerr) and the native girl Liat (France Nuyen), whom he loves but refuses to marry because of their

cultural heritages. The combination of interracial love with a spy plot keeps the action moving, and the cast is generally competent, though none but Gaynor are musical stars.

Josh Logan's direction is the film's chief puzzle. Garish color filters intrude on almost every number, and Logan himself has admitted he botched the job. It's a tribute to the beauty of the score that every melody survives and triumphs over Logan's misguided visual experimentation.

INTERNATIONAL HOUSE (1933) is only an excuse for throwing some of Paramount Studio's best comedians and singers together in an exotic setting, but it is a lot of fun.

The plot revolves around a new invention—the radioscope, which acts as a telephone set. People come from around the world to the town of Wu Hu to bid on the machine. The front desk manager of the International House is played by Franklin Pangborn, the house doctors by George Burns and Gracie Allen, and the Russian representative by Bela Lugosi.

Into this melange drops W.C. Fields (quite literally: he crashes his airplane—"The Spirit of Brooklyn"—into the rooftop restaurant). Fields takes over the film and destroys the hotel in the process.

Many musical numbers are provided via the radioscope. Rudy Vallee sings "Thank Heaven for You" to his love, which turns out to be a megaphone. Baby Rose Marie (later Rose Marie on The Dick Van Dyke Show) sings and tap-dances on the piano, and the most bizarre number has Cab Calloway singing "Reefer Man." As a revue *International House* is one of the best, high spirited and inventive.

Maria (Julie Andrews) takes the Von Trapp children up into the Austrian Alps to show them that the hills are alive with The Sound of Music. *The film featured simple choreography uplifted by the stunning locales.*

THE ROAD TO BALI (1952) is the best of the Road pictures, a series of films in which Bob Hope and Bing Crosby traveled around the world in search of adventure and Dorothy Lamour. Nothing but an excuse for songs and gags, the film clearly shows the strengths and weaknesses of this long-running series.

The Road pictures depended on three things: nonstop bantering jokes, exotic locales, and sex. The jokes are provided by Hope and Crosby, with scarcely a straight line between them. (When Hope introduces himself to Dorothy Lamour he says he's a "Sportsman, raconteur, polo player, and all around good egg." Crosby quips, "Well don't lay it here.") The exotic locales are studio-built, with little relation to reality. But they do make it easy to show scantily-clad

women. Dorothy Lamour appears in even skimpier dresses.

The many musical numbers are not treated seriously at all. In one large production number the native girls do an Oriental dance, and then Crosby and Hope appear wearing kilts and playing bagpipes. They do a spirited dance, but aren't they in the wrong picture? No. This film doesn't care about logic or accuracy, and it is this improvisational nature that audiences at the time loved.

SILK STOCKINGS (1957) is the perfect cold war musical, taking America's every fear about Russia and putting it on the screen. But, as expected, Russia is no match for Fred Astaire.

Russia is represented by Ninotchka (Cyd Charisse), a cold, aloof, almost asexual woman. Constantly spouting propaganda, she has been conditioned to reject the comforts of life (because they are unavailable in Russia). When she checks into a hotel room, she asks which part of the room is hers. Her adversary, Steven Canfield (Astaire) is America embodied: a slick, hedonistic, film producer who takes nothing seriously. Paris is the arena for these two super powers. Through their clashes they fall in love.

The musical numbers also demonstrate the cold war attitude. Astaire sings "Paris Loves Lovers," while Charisse in counterpoint accuses Astaire of being "Capitalistic and Imperialistic." A trio of

Bob Hope, Bing Crosby, and Dorothy Lamour find that The Road to Bali *requires only semi-formal attire.*

Russian officers, including Jules Munshin and Peter Lorre (in his only singing role), sings about the joy of "Siberia" where you can be sure "your Christmas will be white" and everyone boogies to "The Red Blues."

Cole Porter wrote some of his best capitalistic tunes for *Silk Stockings*. In "All of You," which Astaire sings to Charisse, the censors did not let him say "I'd like to make a tour of you," but approved of him loving "the east, west, north and the south of you." A lovely dance between Charisse and Astaire follows, resembling the Astaire-Rogers seduction dances. Another beautiful number is Charisse's solo to "Silk Stockings," in which she changes from a severe Russian outfit into beautiful, decadent clothes, including silk stockings.

WEEKEND IN HAVANA (1941) demonstrates the talents of Alice Faye. She is able to turn even a dumb movie into something special. Faye is aided by another 20th Century Fox regular, the weird Carmen Miranda. Together they make one long for the pre-Castro days in Cuba, when everyone sang and danced and was happy all day long.

The contrast between the languid Faye and the energetic Miranda is one of the reasons they work well together. They split the musical duties between them. Faye sings "Tropical Magic," which celebrates the lush Cuban setting. Miranda's numbers, on the other hand, celebrate sex in the lush surroundings. One song explains that she may say no, but there's "si, si in my eyes."

Other cast members have mostly thankless jobs. John Payne, as the man who is supposedly after Faye, plays a character who is very square and very awkward around women. The Latins, however, as represented by Caesar Romero are all sensual and uninhibited. Romero at least is really Cuban, but that is the only authentic thing about the film. Romero is a compulsive gambler who is probably not above stealing. Miranda spends the entire film trying to get him to quit, and then when he actually makes some money she encourages him to keep doing it. Even so, the film is well worth seeing for Miranda's musical numbers alone.

Carmen Miranda performs her nightclub act in Weekend in Havana.

Fred Astaire dances "The Ritz Rock 'n' Roll," combining his stock in trade—top hat and tails—with the more recent musical movement. Silk Stockings was one of Astaire's last dancing roles, and one of his best.

Musicals often transport the viewer to an exotic land. **ON A CLEAR DAY YOU CAN SEE FOREVER** (1970) goes even further, transporting the viewer into a more exotic time period.

Barbra Streisand plays Daisy Gamble, a neurotic, talkative, dull girl, engaged to a dull man who will soon go to work for a dull corporation. But things are not what they seem. Miss Gamble knows when the phone is going to ring. She also knows when people are thinking about her, and she can make plants grow quickly. To get to the bottom of this, Dr. Mark Chabot, a college profesor (Yves Montand), puts her under hypnosis and discovers that she has another personality—that of Melinda, who lived in 18th-century England. Melinda is sexy, mysterious, and alluring, and Dr. Chabot finds himself falling in love with her. But he can't stand Melinda's current landlord, Daisy.

Jack Nicholson plays Daisy Gamble's stepbrother, who pops in occasionally to give his critique of the work ethic. His character is one of the things that made the film relevant. Bob Newhart has a small but funny part. The administration at Chabot's college is not happy at the attention they get when his students hold a demonstration, and Newhart, as the college president, explains, "In a private academy, academic freedom means that if you disagree with the administration, you're free to go to another academy."

On a Clear Day You Can See Forever is an attempt to make the musical more relevant and "with-it." It deals with parapsychology, college unrest, alternative teaching, and the corporate establishment. The film was made in the late 1960s, when hippies were fashionable and everyone was trying to get on the bandwagon. Though dated, it is still interesting.

FUNNY FACE (1957) teamed Fred Astaire with Audrey Hepburn for a fast-moving musical about the fashion industry. The all-Gershwin score matches the excellent script, making the film irresistible.

Astaire plays Richard Avery, a character loosely based on photographer Richard Avedon. He discovers shy bookworm Audrey Hepburn and decides that she will make a perfect model. They go to Paris to model, and she falls in love with him because he treats her like a woman.

Along the way are many wonderful dances. Astaire does a variation on his cane dance, this time using an umbrella, which somehow becomes a toreador number. Hepburn, wearing all black, does a sizzling beatnik dance for "expressional relief," and in a wonderfully fresh outdoor setting the two have a soaring romantic duet to the tune of "He Loves and She Loves."

The dances are heightened because of the unusually beautiful photography. Richard Avedon was actually responsible for the still pictures of Hepburn shown throughout the film and his influence is seen throughout. The mist-filled sequences of Paris at night are equal in beauty only to the dark and moody interiors of the beatnik cafés that Hepburn haunts.

Photographer Fred Astaire finds it easy to make glamorous photos with Audrey Hepburn as his model. Funny Face both exulted and lightly spoofed the world of high fashion.

Hepburn was frequently teamed against men twice her age, like Humphrey Bogart in *Sabrina*. When Astaire introduced the title song on Broadway in 1927, Audrey Hepburn hadn't even been born yet. *Funny Face* is one of Astaire's greatest musicals; he has made only two more musical films since.

Based on a Broadway show, **ON THE TOWN** (1949) follows the exploits of three sailors sightseeing in New York City on 24-hour passes. This Hollywood film treats New York City as an exotic locale. They see the sights, meet some girls, sing, and dance.

It's pretty hard for a musical like this to go wrong when two of the sailors are Gene Kelly and Frank Sinatra (the third being Jules Munshin). The girls they meet are Ann Miller, Vera-Ellen, and Betty Garrett.

One of the innovations that directors Gene Kelly and Stanley Donen incorporated into *On the Town* was a striking use of location photography. By 1949 Hollywood had become so studio-bound that real locations were a novelty. For a change Kelly and Donen took the cast to the Statue of Liberty to do their singing.

On the Town.

There are two dance highlights in the film: a simple soft shoe to "Main Street" by Gene Kelly and Vera-Ellen, and an elaborate dream ballet in which the six leads meet each other against a stark black and blue Manhattan skyline. The script by Adolph Green and Betty Comden varies from witty to corny. The humor in the film is best summed up in a line spoken by a policeman who has just heard that a dinosaur (skeleton) has collapsed: "I always liked that Dinah Shore."

AN AMERICAN IN PARIS

(1951) is Gene Kelly and MGM's bid to show that the musical could be serious art.

An American In Paris is a sophisticated variation on the old theme of boy meets girl. Gene Kelly plays Jerry Milligan, an artist living in Paris. He gets a sponsor, Milo Roberts (Nina Foch) who may be interested in buying more than Mulligan's paintings. At the same time, Mulligan meets and falls in love with Lise Bourvier (Leslie Caron), who is engaged to Henri Baurel (Georges Guetary), who rescued her family during the war. She owes her allegiance to Baurel and cannot break the engagement, even though she does not love him.

The sophisticated variation is that although boy loses girl, boy does not get girl in the plot proper, but in the fantasy finale.

Although Bourvier loves Mulligan, she leaves, and he fantasies the 17½-minute "An American in Paris" ballet. The ballet opens with a cartoon-like scene of Paris, with the Arc de Triomphe in the distance and cardboard streetlights in the foreground. Color is added to the backdrop, and then people. The impact of seeing 3-dimensional people running around 2-dimensional sets is stunning. As the dance intensifies, the sets become more realistic. One scene is done in pastels, another in watercolors. But while the sets designed by Irene Sharaff are great, the dancing is subdued and uninventive.

Stripped of its music, *An American In Paris* would be intolerable. The story tries to be world-weary and jaded, showing the corruption of art, but it does not go far enough. Milo, though attracted to Mulligan, seems sincere in her appreciation of his art, and it is Mulligan who looks opportunistic when he makes a pass at her. And because the film is so sophisticated it contains no levity. It is either carefully calculated clowning around or dead seriousness.

Producer Arthur Freed and director Vincente Minnelli set out to make a musical that would be critically acclaimed as a serious film, and *An American In Paris* was lavished with praise, culminating in an Academy Award for best picture and an honorary award for Gene Kelly.

Leslie Caron in the spectacular final sequence ballet from An American in Paris. Gene Kelly discovered ballet dancer Caron in Paris and cast her in the lead role for her film debut.

FIDDLER ON THE ROOF (1971) is the film version of one of the most successful Broadway musicals ever staged. It tells the story of a Jewish village in turn-of-the-century Russia, focusing on one family with five daughters. Based on stories by Sholem Aleichem, *Fiddler On The Roof* concerns Tevye, a poor milkman who suffers constantly but is buoyed by his sense of humor. During the course of the film, he is tested to his limit. His first daughter refuses to marry her intended, the second marries without his consent, and the third marries a non-Jew. The final tragedy comes when all the Jews are forced to evacuate their little town.

The book by Joseph Stein perfectly captures the Jewish spirit. There are many jokes, but there is an underlying pain evident in quips like "When a poor man eats a chicken, one of the two is sick." The superior score is full of "Old World" flavor. "If I Were a Rich Man" contains the philosophy that wealth bestows instant wisdom, and sets the tone for the film with a mixture of poignancy and humor.

The mixture of humor and pain is central to Tevye's character, although Topol, an Israeli actor, is a little too serious for the role; instead of bearing suffering through humor, he seems to bear suffering because he is a masochist.

In My Fair Lady, *Professor Henry Higgins boasts to Colonel Pickering that he can turn any street urchin into a lady, as street urchin Eliza Doolittle listens in.*

MY FAIR LADY (1964) represents the musical at its best. Witty, elegant and tuneful, the show is a classic. It is based on George Bernard Shaw's *Pygmalion*, in which a language teacher named Henry Higgins takes a street girl and passes her off as a countess after language training. He picks Eliza Doolittle, subjects her to grueling training, and then falls in love with her.

A lecture on the different dialects people speak may not seem promising as a song, but Lerner and Loewe's "Why Can't the English Teach Their Children How to Speak?" is delightful. Another unlikely musical number has become a classic: in the middle of an all-night session, when everyone is thoroughly exhausted, Eliza breaks out with a perfectly pronounced "The Rain in Spain Stays Mainly in the Plain." And this great musical number dramatizes her linguistic triumph. Soon after this, she revels in her achievement by attending a society party and sings "I Could Have Danced All Night."

Rex Harrison was born to play Henry Higgins. Aloof, hyperlogical, unfeeling, and at the same time childish and irrational, he is lovable and hateful at the same time. He finally becomes emotional after Eliza has gone away. He realizes that he loves her and sings "I've Grown Accustomed to Her Face."

My Fair Lady suffers somewhat by being too faithful to the stage show; it should have been cut judiciously. The film begins to drag toward the end. Not a line was cut from this classic show. While a better movie was possible, *My Fair Lady* is so good it remains a great movie musical.

Charles Dickens' *Oliver Twist* is the dark and grim tale of an orphan forced into thievery in Victorian London. Making a musical version of this tale that is both a faithful retelling and a joyous song celebration is

quite a feat. **OLIVER!** (1968) does not gloss over Dickens' darkness—there are long dramatic passages that bring the London underworld to life in all its infamy. But the film is able to add a new dimension to the story by encasing the hopes and aspirations of the characters in song and dance.

Oliver! overwhelms the senses with its large cast and epic quality. Major events of the story are accompanied by lavish production numbers whose spectacle conveys Oliver's wonder. Oliver (Mark Lester) is an orphan in a dreary state orphanage who causes an uproar when he dares to ask for more porridge. He is sold and runs away when his new masters mistreat him. In London he meets the pickpocket Artful Dodger (Jack Wild). The Dodger befriends him and allows him to join his enclave of boy thieves, which is run by the crafty Fagin (Ron Moody). Oliver eventually discovers his true parentage and leaves the pickpockets' life, but not before becoming entangled in the schemes of the nasty crook Bill Sykes (Oliver Reed).

Oliver! shows what a collaborative effort a film really is. Director Carol Reed gets credit for coordinating this massive project, but each element shines on its own. The art direction is superb, bringing Victorian London to the screen in a wealth of detail: from the bandits' lair to the large marketplace, each set is just right. The songs are catchy, but so well-integrated into the story that they tend not to call attention to themselves. The production numbers are among the biggest ever filmed.

But the most important contribution to *Oliver!* were the performances. Mark Lester is truly appealing as the innocent Oliver. Ron Moody's Fagin is as memorable for his tenderness as Oliver Reed's Bill Sykes is for his brutality. *Oliver!* was justly showered with five Academy Awards, including best picture.

Oliver (Mark Lester) arrives in London to be sold by his cruel orphanage-keeper.

TOP HAT (1935) is the definitive Fred Astaire-Ginger Rogers film. A fantasy about the rich, it provided the perfect setting for romance, dancing, and a glimpse of heaven for Depression-time America.

Like many Astaire-Rogers films, the plot hinges flimsily on mistaken identity. Fred Astaire is a professional dancer in the show of his pal, Edward Everett Horton. Astaire is crazy about a girl he met in a hotel, and he chases her to Venice. However, Ginger thinks that he is Horton, the husband of her best friend, and she refuses his adulterous entreaties until the end of the film.

Fred's discovery of Ginger is cleverly worked into one of Astaire's solo dances. In his hotel room Astaire does what he always does—tap-dance on the fireplace, serve drinks in rhythm, and stomp on the floor, but little does he realize that practically beneath his feet, in the room below, is Ginger Rogers in a huge satin bed trying to sleep. When she confronts Astaire, he promises to stop, then sprinkles sand on the floor and lightly does a sand shuffle to put her to sleep.

Fred and Ginger enjoy an intimate tango dip as they make love in movement.

"Cheek to Cheek" is sheer perfection. Rogers dances this number dressed in a white feathery dress that sheds. The dance starts slowly, builds with Astaire vaulting Rogers up into the air, her dress billowing, and slows as Astaire brings Rogers down to earth, her back arched in his arms. He gently lifts her up and dances away.

In another classic Astaire solo, he sings "Top Hat, White Tie, and Tails." Behind him is a chorus of men wearing the outfit described in the title, white carnations, and carrying canes. They match Astaire's steps then leave him to dance with his cane, beating out one rhythm with the cane, tapping another with his foot. Then he turns the cane into a lethal weapon as the chorus lines up, and he shoots them using only his cane and his taps.

FLYING DOWN TO RIO (1933) may be the most spectacular case of scene-stealing in movie history. It stars Dolores Del Rio, Gene Raymond, and Raoul Roulien in a half-hearted tale of a pilot vying for the affections of a singer against a band leader. But no one ever notices them, because this is the film that introduced Fred Astaire and Ginger Rogers. Their minor roles in this film were enough to make them stars.

There is only one Astaire-Rogers dance in *Flying Down to Rio*, but that is The Carioca, which became a nationwide dance craze. The dance, invented by Hermes Pan (an old friend of Astaire's), is a fast tango done by dancing forehead to forehead, hands clasped overhead. In the scene, Astaire explains it as mental telepathy; then, after watching the supposedly amateur dancers do it, he and Ginger give it a crack. They go to center stage, which consists of seven white pianos pushed together, and do their variations. Compared to the ensemble dancing that has just preceded them, they are a breath of fresh air, totally free and relaxed. When they knock their heads together they stagger back, dazed, trying to find each other. Rogers lifts her skirts to perform a Latin tap, and Astaire matches it. There is one prolonged moment where they stand face to face softly tapping, grinning at each other in total joy. No one had ever made dancing look this easy and this much fun.

Fred Astaire and his male chorus sing the glories of a "Top Hat, White Tie, and Tails." *Top Hat* is one of the best Fred Astaire-Ginger Rogers vehicles.

THE BEST OF ROCK 'N' ROLL

THE BUDDY HOLLY STORY (1978)
HAIR (1979)
THE GIRL CAN'T HELP IT (1956)
JAILHOUSE ROCK (1957)
A HARD DAY'S NIGHT (1964)
HELP! (1965)
YELLOW SUBMARINE (1968)
LET IT BE (1970)
ROCK 'N' ROLL HIGH SCHOOL (1979)
TOMMY (1975)
QUADROPHENIA (1979)
THE WALL (1982)
JESUS CHRIST SUPERSTAR (1973)

"It happens out in Vegas, happens in Moline
On the blue blood streets of Boston
Up in Berkeley and out in Queens."

"The Fire Down Below"
Bob Seger

Elvis Presley and Ann-Margret spin their wheels for some kicks in Viva Las Vegas. Elvis' tough guy persona was inexplicably watered down in the movies, which accounts for the Vespa instead of a Harley between his legs here.

THE BUDDY HOLLY STORY (1978) is one of the few movies concerned with rock music as well as rock performers. The texture, mechanics, and feeling of rock music are all central to the film, because they were central to Buddy Holly's life. By providing insight into rock music, the film offers insight into Buddy Holly, who comes across as a real human being.

The film begins in 1958 at a Lubbock, Texas roller rink. Buddy Holly and his band are being broadcast over the radio. Holly's heart is not in it when he sings slow numbers like "Mockingbird Hill," so he plays one of his own creations— "That'll Be the Day." The effect is electrifying, and all the previously bored kids spring to life, crowding the stage and dancing. But Lubbock is not ready for Holly's music. Radio sponsors insist he be barred and preachers denounce his music as "un-Christian and un-American jungle rhythms— a threat to our morals."

Buddy soon achieves success. He is interrupted in the midst of a rehearsal to be told that he has a hit record. His DJ friend sent a tape of the roller rink concert to a New York record company, who accidentally released it as a single. The company is so in awe of Holly's sound that his group, the Crickets, gets a contract with an unheard-of clause making Holly producer of his own records. Subsequently, all the real drama occurs in the recording studio. Holly hires string players to flesh out his music, he discovers over-dubbing, and he creates a new sound.

Each new song is not only entertaining, but also shows Holly's development, a dual function that makes the songs more compelling. "It's So Easy to Fall in Love," "Oh Boy," and "Words of Love" all are good songs, made better by the context.

Because so much emphasis is placed on the music, there isn't time to indulge in the usual musical biography clichés. In Holly's presuccess days, where such films typically foreshadow greatness, Holly is just another nerdish-looking boy from Texas. His parents are equally unstereotyped. They have no objections to his starting a rock band; they just want him "to have something to fall back on." Everything is deglamorized. The group takes its name from a cricket that messes up their first recording session in Holly's garage. These are all things that happen to real people, not superstars.

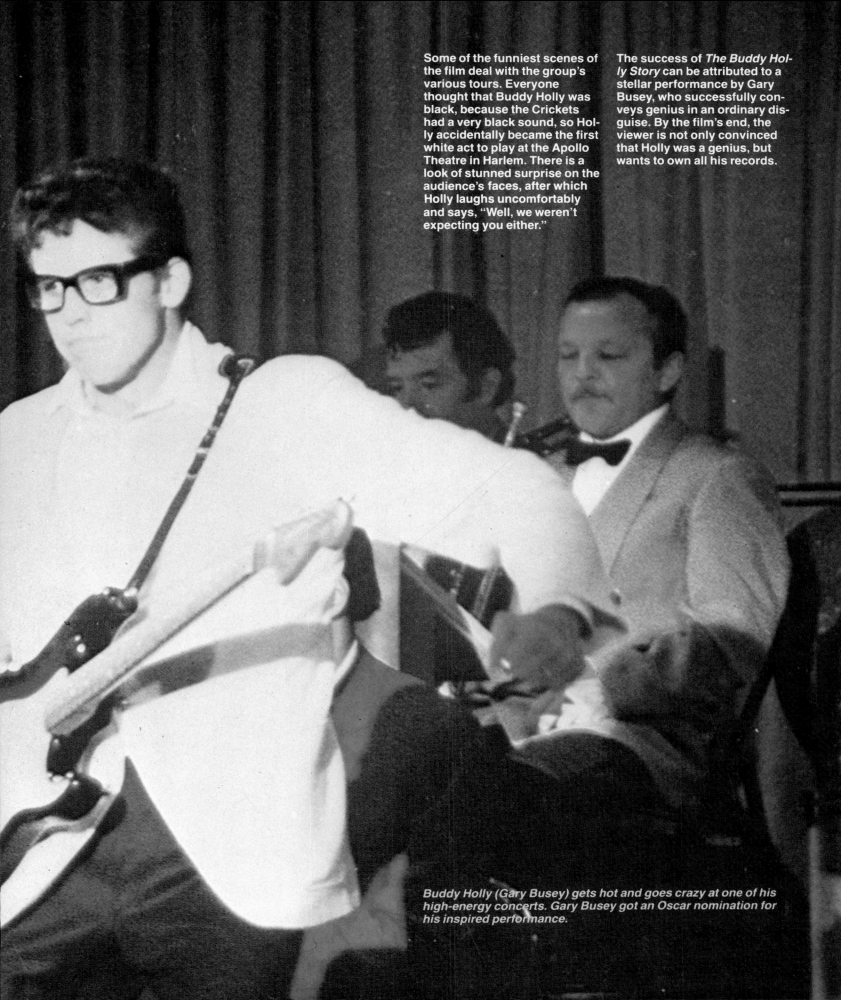

Some of the funniest scenes of the film deal with the group's various tours. Everyone thought that Buddy Holly was black, because the Crickets had a very black sound, so Holly accidentally became the first white act to play at the Apollo Theatre in Harlem. There is a look of stunned surprise on the audience's faces, after which Holly laughs uncomfortably and says, "Well, we weren't expecting you either."

The success of *The Buddy Holly Story* can be attributed to a stellar performance by Gary Busey, who successfully conveys genius in an ordinary disguise. By the film's end, the viewer is not only convinced that Holly was a genius, but wants to own all his records.

Buddy Holly (Gary Busey) gets hot and goes crazy at one of his high-energy concerts. Gary Busey got an Oscar nomination for his inspired performance.

HAIR (1979) is the musical they said couldn't be made. The Broadway show on which it is based had been a phenomenally successful 1960s cultural artifact that idealized controversial, provocative hippies. But the play became dated, just as the hippies did. Director Milos Forman's problem was how to transfer an old topical play to the screen with the benefit of hindsight. The result was *Hair*, a film that reinterprets the hippies while still portraying them sympathetically and remaining faithful to the spirit of the musical.

Playwright Michael Weller wrote the screenplay for *Hair*. It was a completely original script because the play had been a plotless revue. At the same time, the story had to be structured around the songs. Weller fashioned a story around Claude Hooper Bukowski (John Savage), an Oklahoma boy who has been drafted and meets some hippies on his way to the induction center. The hippies are portrayed as a fun-loving, freewheeling group with their cries for free love, free drugs, and freedom. While the screenplay can make one nostalgic for the hippies, it does not glorify them. Their vague concept of freedom is fine until it is revealed that one of the hippies has deserted his wife and kids in pursuit of independence.

After the group is arrested, Berger (Treat Williams) must raise bail money from his mother, a scene which makes the point that these people often had access to money, which allowed them to indulge in the luxury of playing poor without suffering the consequences.

Twyla Tharp choreographed the vibrant dances, each of which is spectacular in its own way. "Aquarius," the ode to the new age, immediately sets the tone for the film. In Central Park, a ramshackle group of hippies gather around the lead singer. As she sings about the astrological configurations that will lead to "harmony and understanding," the camera quickly spins around her, revealing the greenery, and then everyone joins in a wild dance. In a charming moment

two hippies kick their legs out, and two mounted policemen's horses imitate the step; the hippies step to the right, and the horses follow. There is life, there is whimsy, there is love in this dance, the perfect introduction to the hippies.

The songs are often given new meanings through their placement in the film. "Black Boys/White Boys," which was sung in the show by a chorus of white women, extolled the sexual virtues of black men; it was used to symbolize racial understanding. In the film the girls are still there, but they are joined by a trio of army recruiting officers staring at their naked recruits. It is impudent but effective, and the song is used well.

Credit for *Hair*'s contemporary look goes to director Milos Forman. "Black Boys/White Boys" is a good example of his editing style: he juxtaposes the hippie girls singing in the park with the army men singing in the office. Though they are not physically near each other, a type of duet is formed through the cutting, and it is very effective.

The score by Gerome Ragni, James Rado, and Galt MacDermot contains many gems. "Good Morning Starshine," with its silly lyrics and lilting melody, is charming. "Easy to be Hard" is a poignant song that laments the inability of people to feel. Even "3-5-0-0," a sinister anti-Vietnam song, still works. If all this were not enough, *Hair* has a truly great cast. Treat Williams sings, dances, and acts with an impish, anti-establishment glee. John Savage is convincingly innocent (his conversion to the hippie's way of life is extremely effective), and Beverly D'Angelo brings beauty and grace to her role as the upper-class debutante.

Hair functions well as a work of intelligent nostalgia, which is quite an achievement.

Hair *director Milos Forman set most of the action outdoors in order to downplay familiar hippie artifacts and stress the counterculture credo of freedom.*

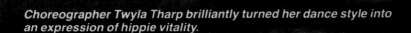

Choreographer Twyla Tharp brilliantly turned her dance style into an expression of hippie vitality.

THE GIRL CAN'T HELP IT (1956) is really two films in one: it is a sexually obsessed and repressed comedy typical of the 1950s (like *Some Like It Hot*), and it is one of the best early rock 'n' roll films. Though the plot doesn't revolve around teenagers, and the show business world depicted is far removed from rock 'n' roll, *The Girl Can't Help It* manages to cram 17 tunes into its 99 minutes. There are excellent performances by Little Richard, Fats Domino, Gene Vincent, The Platters, Eddie Cochran, and Ray Anthony and the Imperials. The acts occur in the backdrop of the story, but they are presented with visual imagination and respect.

Jayne Mansfield plays a blonde bombshell named Jerri Jordan whose boyfriend Murdock (Edmond O'Brien) wants to turn her into a singer. Jerri doesn't want a career; she wants to settle down with a husband and family. When Murdock hires agent Tom Miller (Tom Ewell) to manage her career, Jerri fakes an inability to sing. In this cynical look at show business, an inability to sing can't stop a career, especially when the "talent" has a body like Mansfield's. While trying to mold her singing career around her handicap, Tom and Jerri fall in love. This is a problem because Murdock is a former mobster with a nasty temper, and not a guy to take jilting lightly.

The musical numbers in the film are the high points, and there are many. They run the gamut from reality to fantasy in the manner of their presentations. Julie London sings a fantasy number in which she plays herself come back in a dream to haunt her former agent Tom Miller. No matter where he turns, she reappears in front of him (in a new dress each time), singing "Cry Me a River." Eddie Cochran's number appears on a television set on *The Ed Sullivan Show.* There is even a hilarious song for the non-singing Jerri—a chorus performs the lyrics while Jerri punctuates the songs with screams. An obscure rock 'n' roll trio named

The Chuckles nearly steal the show with their song "Cinnamon Sinner."

The Girl Can't Help It doesn't seem to know much about the context of rock 'n' roll, but it presents more of it more entertainingly than the teen-pics of the time that purported to be rock 'n' roll musicals.

The story of Elvis Presley and his movies is a tragic one indeed. Presley had one of the most dynamic personalities ever to hit the music scene, with a raw energy that could devastate audiences. Yet that energy was invariably wasted in his films. Elvis didn't seem to care, nor did his fans, who

Agent Tom Miller (Tom Ewell) wows the New York nightclub scene with Jerri Jordan's (Jayne Mansfield) excellent posture in The Girl Can't Help It.

would sit through any movie to see their hero. As a result, only a few of Presley's thirty films are truly good; of those, JAIL-HOUSE ROCK (1957) is perhaps the best.

Jailhouse Rock is an idealized version of Presley's rise to fame. At the film's beginning, he is a construction worker who accidentally kills a man in a barroom fight and goes to jail. There he shares a cell with a tough con who teaches him a trade. Some cons learn pickpocketing, some learn burglary, but Elvis learns how to play the guitar. After getting out of jail, he starts his own record company, makes millions, and goes to Hollywood. There he becomes a louse, then reforms and discovers the meaning of friendship.

The greatest song in the film is "Jailhouse Rock." The scene opens on a two-tiered prison with all the dancers in their cells hitting the bars in rhythm with their cups. Presley breaks out of his cell and into the song, slides down a firepole, and goes into his hip action as the fast music plays. The others energetically do the Twist, creating an exciting and kinetic number.

The "Jailhouse Rock" dance.

Jailhouse Rock depicts what should have always been Presley's image. He is an unassuming, unrefined man. He kisses a girl suddenly, and when she disapproves of his "tactics," he responds "That ain't tactics, that's just the beast in me." He is often shy, but he is not afraid to fight. He is rebellious, but only when wronged. A record executive steals his song, so Presley beats him up.

Jailhouse Rock was followed in 1958 by *King Creole*, which was Presley's best acting job, though not a musical. Perhaps if one of his films had done poorly, movie executives might have tried to find a good script for Elvis. But people kept coming to see such films as *It Happened at the World's Fair*, in which Presley takes a cute Chinese toddler around the Seattle World's Fair, or *Spinout*, in which he plays a racing car driver/rock singer being pursued by three women. There are occasional good moments in his films, like the title song in *Girls! Girls! Girls!*, with Presley teaching girls the Twist, or his go-go dancing rendition of "Viva Las Vegas" with kitten rocker Ann-Margret, but for the most part his films are painful to watch.

Elvis Presley and Ann-Margret practice their go-go in Viva Las Vegas.

The Beatles took America by storm in 1964. First there was their single "I Wanna Hold Your Hand," then their first American concert, and finally **A HARD DAY'S NIGHT** (1964), their first movie.

A Hard Day's Night tells the story of a day in the life of the Beatles. In an episodic fashion it shows the Beatles fleeing their overenthusiastic fans, some incidents on a train, and the arrival of Paul's grandfather. The grandfather seems innocent enough, but causes trouble—picking up girls, telling Ringo how short he is and that he's unappreciated, and generally creating a nuisance —until all conclude that, "He's just a dirty old man from Liverpool." After a few more incidents, including Ringo's running away from the group, they perform one concert and are whisked away for the next.

The surprise of *A Hard Day's Night* was that the Beatles were extremely likeable actors. With a low-key delivery, the jokes came fast and furious. Even people who didn't like the Beatles' music were won over by their acting. One didn't have to know who the Beatles were in order to appreciate their films, but for those who did, the songs were the drawing card.

The major innovation in the Beatles' films concerned the filming of the musical numbers. Director Richard Lester's approach was to play the song over incongruous images. For example, in **HELP!** (1965), "Ticket to Ride" is on the soundtrack. The corresponding visual is the Beatles clowning around in the snow, riding on snowmobiles, falling down, rolling toward the camera, and sitting on a grand piano that

Yellow Submarine is a psychedelic cartoon using Beatle songs and characters and the pop style of Peter Max.

happens to be there. The shots are rapidly edited in time to the music and come across with a free and improvised quality. No attempt is made to link the song with the story. It is time for the Beatles to play, and it is acknowledged as such. A variation on this approach is found in "Hey, You've Got to

116

Hide Your Love Away," also from *Help!*. The Beatles are shown playing the song, but every attempt is made to break up the images. The scene was shot with several cameras and pieced together from different perspectives, with camera tricks like fast motion and quick zooms. Many copied the style, but few understood it.

But *Help!* also has a plot; it is an insane comedy thriller centering around Ringo's ring. Eastern religious cultists, led by Clang (Leo McKern), want the ring because it plays an important part in their religious sacrifice. Mad scientist Foot (Victor Spinetti) and his helper Algernon (Roy Kinnear) want the ring because with it they can rule the world.

Help!'s style is established early. On a very typical London row of flats, the Beatles enter their house as neighbors across the street comment on how nice it is that success hasn't gone to their heads. Inside, the Beatles casually go about their business. A stranger mows grass using chattering teeth, Ringo goes to a line of soda machines and automat vendors in the back, and Paul rises from the floor playing a neon organ. All of this weird activity is shown casually and deadpan. Several attempts on Ringo's ring follow, each one more wacky and absurd than its predecessor. The end of *Help!* explains everything (or nothing, depending on one's point of view). During the middle of a sprawling scene, the camera tracks back and the title appears, "This film is respectfully dedicated to the memory of Mr. Elias Howe who in 1846 invented the sewing machine."

Help!'s crazy quality is a direct offshoot from a popular British comedy group called The Goons. The Goons, who included Peter Sellers and Spike Milligan, specialized in anarchic comedy, making fun of radio (their medium), while at the same time indulging in terrible puns and strange *non sequiturs*. Their influence can be found in most British comedy, including Monty Python and director Richard Lester.

The Beatles only supplied the music for their next feature, **YELLOW SUBMARINE**, (1968) a strikingly animated film with some of their best songs. The film is the story of Pepperland, a land of all things good and wonderful, led by Sgt. Pepper's Lonely Hearts Club Band. Pepperland is invaded by the Blue Meanies. Only the Beatles can save Pepperland, and the Yellow Submarine is dispatched for them. They save the day.

Pepperland is filled with gay colors out of a Peter Max poster and populated by people designed around nineteenth-century photographs. Each musical number is perfectly realized. "Lucy in the Sky with Diamonds" is appropriately psychedelic. "Eleanor Rigby" with its refrain, "Ah, look at all the lonely people" presents a dreary picture of London with grey/blue buildings, and characters trapped forever in a dull existence.

Yellow Submarine was the Beatles' last musical together. The time and expense that went into making a film were one factor, but the strain of success was the key. In **LET IT BE** (1970), a documentary about the recording sessions for their last album, it is evident that the group is about to split up. Tempers are constantly flaring. Perhaps it is just as well that they quit films early. They had reached the top with nowhere to go but down.

In Help!, *Paul McCartney manages to sing in an open field, despite the explosive military maneuvers of the British Army going on about him.*

Riff's gym class helps her try out her new song, "Rock 'n' Roll High School."

ROCK 'N' ROLL HIGH SCHOOL (1979) is a sophisticated throwback to the rock films that were made in the 1960s. In those loose and stupid films, the story stopped when the band played and the band got out of the way when it was time for the plot. *Rock 'n' Roll High School* recaptures the fun of those pictures, without sinking to their level.

Vince Lombardi High School, where the students care only about rock 'n' roll, is the setting. The student who dances the most is Riff Randall, whose only goal in life is to get the Ramones to sing a song she has written. The Ramones come to town to give a concert and do their schtick, which is eating greasy pizza. Miss Togar, the new principal, tries to stop the concert. The students rebel and take over the high school. The film ends in song as the high school is blown up.

In order to get Ramones tickets Riff cuts school for three days, blaming each absence on the death of her mother, her father, and finally her goldfish. When Miss Togar's spies, Fritz Hansel and Fritz Gretel, gleefully return with Riff's goldfish, Miss Togar snarls, "I'm sure her parents are alive, too."

The jokes serve as good filler between the songs. There is an energetic dance to "Rock 'n' Roll High School" in the school gym, and a sequence in which Riff fantasizes about the Ramones. She finds a Ramone in her shower, in her closet, and in her bed. The film concludes with a Ramones concert. *Rock 'n' Roll High School* does sag after the first hour, but comedies are hard to sustain, and it is entertaining enough to make up for that.

The cast is fresh and engaging. P. J. Soles (of *Halloween* fame) plays Riff Randall. Clint Howard (Ron Howard's brother) is particularly swarmy as Eaglebauer, an entrepreneurial student. Stellar performances are delivered by Mary Woronov as the evil Miss Togar, and Paul Bartel as Mr. McGree the math teacher.

Roger Corman produced *Rock 'n' Roll High School*, and the film clearly bears his stamp. Corman pioneered the low-budget film. He was a master at satisfying his audience with a mixture of sex, horror, violence, or whatever was in vogue. By anticipating and creating movie tastes Corman made huge profits and churned out films on a regular basis. Corman built a truly independent small studio, which he used to train new directors. As long as their films came in on budget they were allowed free rein. This was not mere altruism. Francis Ford Coppola (*Dementia 13*), Martin Scorcese (*Box Car Bertha*), Peter Bogdanovich (*Targets*), Jonathan Demme (*Caged Heat*), and many others cut their celluloid teeth under Corman's watchful eye. *Rock 'n' Roll High School* is a direct result of this policy. It is high class schlock.

Riff Randall (P.J. Soles) thinks The Ramones are just "Gabba Gabba Hey!" The Ramones themselves, of course, simply "don't want to be a pinhead no more." The speech of these rockers is subtitled for those who need help.

Tommy-the-record is amusing and light with its "use the force" instinctual approach to pinball. *Tommy*-the-movie is pretentious and weighty. Director Ken Russell has a history of thwarting writers and imposing his vision on material no matter what the consequences. Because *Tommy* was not written to be staged, much of the action is only vaguely implied by the songs. To film

Perhaps the most destructive thing Russell does to *Tommy* is give it religious significance. There is a belabored parallel between Tommy and Christ. When he is with Acid Queen Tina Turner, he is dressed like Christ on the cross, complete with a crown of bloody flowers (instead of thorns). When Tommy goes to a faith ministry, it is the Church of Marilyn Monroe, where they worship a huge plaster replica of Monroe in a pose from *The Seven Year Itch*. As a story of leadership a certain amount of religious parody is appropriate, but Russell uses it at all the wrong times.

Roger Daltry plays Tommy with perfect wide-eyed optimism and innocence, Ann-Margret (as Tommy's mother) gets to cry a lot, Keith Moon is delightfully perverted as Uncle Ernie, and Tina Turner is excellent as the Acid Queen. The singing is good, and Elton John gives a good rendition of "Pinball Wizard," although the music is over-orchestrated. There are many other musical highlights, but *Tommy* remains a movie at odds with itself, and the sum of the parts is greater than the whole.

TOMMY (1975) is based on The Who's classic 1969 rock opera. A parody of leader worship, it concerns Tommy, who as a child witnessed the murder of his father. Tommy is psychologically struck deaf, dumb, and blind, and he stays that way for a long time. In his helpless state, he is much abused until he discovers his true vocation, playing pinball. He becomes a celebrity because of his high scores, and at the pinnacle of his fame he regains his sight and hearing. Tommy becomes a cult leader and starts Tommy camps where people come seeking intellectual fulfillment. The answer Tommy preaches is pinball, and the people are made deaf, dumb, and blind in order for their pinball instincts to surface. His followers finally get restless and rebel against Tommy. As everything falls apart, Tommy escapes.

Tommy, dramatic sense had to be created from the songs, and the plot had to be clarified. Russell did this, but gave the story a different meaning than might reasonably be inferred from the record. Frequently he puts incongruous images on the screen to change the effect of the songs. In "I'm Free," Tommy strips his mother of her jewelry, throwing it into the sea. This action makes no sense in the context of the song.

QUADROPHENIA (1979) is the most intelligent rock-album-to-movie adaptation yet made. Several rock albums have been filmed, but the songs have usually not been strong enough dramatically to carry the film. *Quadrophenia* functions as a real film. Instead of pointless images and meaningless political rhetoric, it projects clearly drawn characters and a real feeling for a turbulent time.

The film takes place in London during the early 1960s. Jim Cooper (Phil Daniels) is the Quadropheniac. On the record, Quadrophenia is defined as intense schizophrenia with four personalities instead of just two. Cooper may be misdiagnosed in the film, but he clearly does not know what he is doing or what he wants. He has a dead end job and an unsupportive family, and he gets the most fun out of popping pills and riding his scooter. He desperately seeks affiliation with something, and becomes a Mod. Mods dress cool, Mods listen to The Who, Mods are future-oriented, and Mods hate Rockers (called Greasers in America) who are into the 1950s. When Jim is with the Mods, his Mod personality takes over, and when one of

his best friends is pummeled by the Mods because he may be a Rocker, Jim only walks away.

The focal point of the movie is a sequence in Brighton. Thousands of youths from around the country make a pilgrimage there, and Jim has the time of his life. He wins the respect of Ace-Face (the coolest of the Mods), beats up some Rockers in a huge riot, makes love in a dirty alley to the girl of his dreams, and is also

arrested. In the final third of the film, Jim loses everything: his job, his girl, his bike, and his family. Whatever ideals Jim has left are shattered when he discovers that in the real world Ace-Face (Sting of The Police) is nothing but a hotel bellboy. Totally disillusioned, he steals Ace-Face's bike and rides away, casting off his past.

Quadrophenia is uncompromising in its examination of British youth. If The Who were interested only in delighting their fans, they would have made a film about kids rebelling against their bourgeois parents and trying to remake society; the kids would have been heroes. But *Quadrophenia* is more realistic. The world is complex, without heroes and without answers.

While society may be bad, the kids mirror it, and are just as cold, blind, and unfeeling as their parents.

The music is utilized beautifully in the film. The songs from the *Quadrophenia* album are employed with great restraint at the right moments. Period songs pepper the film to provide a frame of reference. At the beginning, while Jim cruises on his motorcycle, a song asks, "Can You See the Real Me?" There are no songs during the whole Brighton episode because it would break the dramatic flow, but when the audience needs time to reflect on what has happened, "5:15" provides a pause.

Unfortunately, *Quadrophenia* was labelled too quickly as a rock musical and few outsiders gave the film a chance. It deserves to be seen as an example of the potential of the rock film.

Tommy (Roger Daltrey) strikes one of his many Christ-like poses. While the idol-parody is a little heavy-handed, the original rock songs by The Who are quite good.

Pink (Bob Geldof) watches his favorite nihilistic TV program in The Wall.

The stunning animation in The Wall.

Pink Floyd's **THE WALL** (1982) is the most recent rock album to be adapted into a movie. The film is designed primarily for Pink Floyd fans, and they will be pleased because it clarifies the enigmatic songs.

The Wall opens with a lot of jumbled imagery. A man sits in his hotel room watching television, a child runs through army trenches lined with decaying corpses, and a mob of teenagers riots in front of a stadium where there is going to be a rock concert. Eventually the images come together. The child is the rock singer, alienated and alone in his hotel room. The riot is occurring at

his concert. His name is listed as Pink, but it's not clear that the band is actually supposed to be Pink Floyd. As the riot escalates, there is a contest between the police and the teenagers to see who can be more brutal.

The film flashes back to Pink's childhood as he sits in a classroom and a nasty old schoolteacher berates him for writing poetry in class. In the musical sequence that follows, the kids sitting at their desks are placed on a conveyor belt. To the strains of "We don't need no education," they are fed into a machine and come out mass-produced.

All of this is in the spirit of Pink Floyd. They are a group concerned with depression and human misery. These themes were brought out in albums like "The Dark Side of the Moon." The music is good, and as there has been no attempt to synchronize it to action, it sounds immediate, but Pink Floyd's *The Wall* is a film for the already converted; it will not gain them any new fans.

The rock opera **JESUS CHRIST SUPERSTAR** (1973) was born as a best-selling record that took England and America by storm, raising controversy with its portrayal of a rock 'n' roll Jesus.

The story concerns Jesus' last week on earth, presented through the perspective of a revisionist Judas. Judas is an intellectual who realizes that Christ is losing control. Judas fears that if the Jews become too unruly the Romans will crush them, and in desperation he turns Jesus in. Christ is sentenced to die, and Judas, wracked with guilt, commits suicide, only to show up later in heaven. Along the way are wonderful songs like "I Don't Know How To Love Him" sung by Mary Magdalene, and the spooky "Pilate's Dream." King Herod steals the picture when he says to Christ, "Prove to me that you're no fool, walk across my swimming pool."

The film has a daring, though not entirely successful concept. A group of actors arrive in Israel to perform the movie, mixing the old and the new. In one scene people dress in Roman garb, and in another a jet is carted out. The point of this, however, is difficult to ascertain. It detracts from the film, as does the bad dubbing, poor orchestration, and dull acting. What the film has going for it are beautiful sets, great music, and a compelling story.

THE MOST UNUSUAL MUSICALS

HEAD (1968)
ONE FROM THE HEART (1982)
CABIN IN THE SKY (1943)
MADAM SATAN (1930)
FOLLOW THE FLEET (1936)
IT'S ALWAYS FAIR WEATHER (1955)
THE ROCKY HORROR PICTURE SHOW (1975)
PHANTOM OF THE PARADISE (1974)
CAN HEIRONYMOUS MERKIN EVER FORGET MERCY
    HUMPPE AND FIND TRUE HAPPINESS? (1969)
THE BOY FRIEND (1971)
PENNIES FROM HEAVEN (1981)
THE ROSE (1979)
LADY SINGS THE BLUES (1972)
COAL MINER'S DAUGHTER (1980)
NASHVILLE (1975)

"Or would you rather swing on a star?
Carry moonbeams home in a jar?"

"Swingin' on a Star"
Johnny Burke and Jimmy Van Heusen

Ken Russell's flair for the odd visual came to full fruition in The
Boyfriend, where he attempted to out-Hollywood Busby Berkeley
with bizarre production numbers.

125

HEAD (1968) was a comeback movie for The Monkees. Like those TV rock stars, the film is disorganized and unoriginal, uses cheap jokes, and has occasional flashes of brilliance.

There are several films lurking in *Head,* each one surfacing briefly. The major one concerns The Monkees as a rock group. Mickey Dolenz, Mike Nesmith, Davy Jones, and Peter Tork introduce themselves by singing that they are "A manufactured image with no philosophies...the money's in, we're made of tin, we're here to give you more." Once they've admitted that they're completely talentless, they try desperately to disprove it. But the songs they sing are lackluster and stupid. Surprisingly, The Monkees choose new songs over their old hits—a big mistake.

Another film in *Head* is a broad, freewheeling parody/comedy. With no apparent motivation, it indulges in parodies of the-kid-who-grows-up-in-the-ghetto-wants-to-be-a-violinist-but-becomes-a-boxer-instead movie, the this-town-ain't-big-enough-for-the-both-of-us movie, and the Indians-are-attacking movie. The Monkees constantly emphasize the unreality of the whole thing by storming off sets, breaking the painted backdrops, and walking around the Hollywood studio.

The final film in *Head,* which desperately tries to break out but cannot, is a good movie. One good dance is performed by Davy Jones, dressed in a white suit and dancing on a black set. Every so often there is a cut, and he is dancing in a black suit in front of a white background. The high point occurs after the dance, when Frank Zappa, walking with a cow, commends him on the dance. "You've worked on your dancing, it shows... doesn't leave much time for your music."

Perhaps the most interesting thing about *Head* are the credits. Bob Rafelson (who, along with Bert Schneider, created The Monkees) directed the film. He went on to direct *Five Easy Pieces* and *The Postman Always Rings Twice.* And Jack Nicholson, the actor and director, wrote what was called a script. *Head* did not work as a comeback film; The Monkees did not come back.

The Monkees find themselves
floating in air at the beginning
of Head, a situation that the entire film often found itself in.

Frannie (Teri Garr) leaves her boyfriend after a fight on their anniversary in One From the Heart. *The visual sumptuousness belies the poignancy of the scene.*

ONE FROM THE HEART (1982) is a sometimes spectacular mess, an awesome spectacle in cinematographic experimentation. What it lacks, ironically, is heart. While this film was billed as a salute to the old Hollywood musicals, it really serves as a gigantic showcase for American Zoetrope's new hardware. That in itself, however, is worth the price of admission.

The story of *One From the Heart* is a simple one. Teri Garr plays Frannie and Frederic Forrest plays Hank, a couple who have lived together in Las Vegas for ten years. She works in a travel agency; he sells automobile parts. She's a woman looking for adventure; he's a hard-working, beer-chugging, t-shirt-and-sneakers kind of guy. On their anniversary, she surprises him with tickets to Bora Bora, and he surprises her by buying a house. Soon they're arguing, separating, and having affairs: Forrest with a beautiful circus girl (Nastassia Kinski), and Garr with a suave stranger (Raul Julia). After these flings, Garr and Forrest get back together again. And that's the film.

This simple plot is played against incredibly complicated and rich sets designed by Dean Tavoularis. The most spectacular set is a hallucinatory strip of Las Vegas, complete with weird, flashing neon signs. The sets are consistently good and provide the major satisfaction from the film.

Nastassia Kinski sings in a martini glass—one of the cutest olives the world has ever seen.

There are two dance numbers in the film. The first, a full-fledged spectacle with Teri Garr, Raul Julia, and a hundred extras jumping around making noise, is unfocused and sloppy. The second is more interesting. Forrest is standing in a used-car lot with Kinski. He walks to a pile of junked cars, waves a baton, and the cars come to life—their horns honking and lights flashing in time to his stick. As a mixture of fantasy and the mundane, it is magical—the sort of moment one expects from a musical.

The film is full of similar isolated, spectacular moments. The opening credits, for example, are beautiful—the camera floats across the icons of casino marquees. Nastassia Kinski offers a beautiful screen image too, but her character, like the others, is lost in the shuffle.

Since none of the characters ever sings, the music, written and sung by Tom Waits and Crystal Gayle, is commentary. The songs tend to pull viewers away from the story and distance them from the already weak characters. Director and producer Francis Ford Coppola has successfully stretched the artificiality of the musical set to its (il)logical limits. While many great musicals have been escapist and dumb, they've never sacrificed the characters to the extent that this unusual film does.

CABIN IN THE SKY (1943) is a warm and engaging musical with a very talented cast. Unfortunately it is an all-black musical written and directed by whites. While the intentions of those making it were good, some strange stereotypes still crept in.

Cabin in the Sky, based on the Broadway musical of the same name, takes place in a mythical Southern town. Little Joe (Eddie "Rochester" Anderson) is a good but weak man who just can't keep from gambling with the boys and avoiding church. Petunia (Ethel Waters) is his suffering wife who prays for his salvation. Her prayers are answered, and a messenger of the Lord, known as The General (Kenneth Spencer), comes to help. Lucifer, Jr. (Rex Ingrams), outraged by this, puts in his bid for Little Joe's soul. He sends Georgia Brown (Lena Horne) to tempt Little Joe. Petunia catches them together in an innocent embrace, and she leaves him. Little Joe becomes a big-time gambler. Petunia tries to reclaim him by vamping. She gets low-down and drinks with the boys. Little Joe gets jealous and takes her back. He vows to be good again, and Petunia concludes that "Happiness Is Jes' a Thing Called Joe."

The story is trite, but Anderson and Waters play their roles with such compassion that one is compelled to care for them. Waters' rendition of "Happiness Is Jes' a Thing Called Joe" can bring one to tears. In a sequence notable for its simplicity, Anderson starts to play his guitar, and Waters sings "Taking a Chance on Love" with a warmth that leaps off the screen.

Cabin in the Sky is director Vincente Minnelli's first film. There are short appearances by Louis Armstrong (as the trumpeter Gabriel), the tap-dance team of Buck and Bubbles, and the Duke Ellington Orchestra.

Watch *Cabin in the Sky* without attacking its every racial flaw. Instead be impressed that the film is as good as it is. From a period when the *New York Times* could write that *"Cabin in the Sky* is . . . an inspiring expression of a simple people's faith in the hereafter," one can't expect *Raisin in the Sun*.

Little Joe (Eddie "Rochester" Anderson) and Petunia (Ethel Waters) strut their stuff.

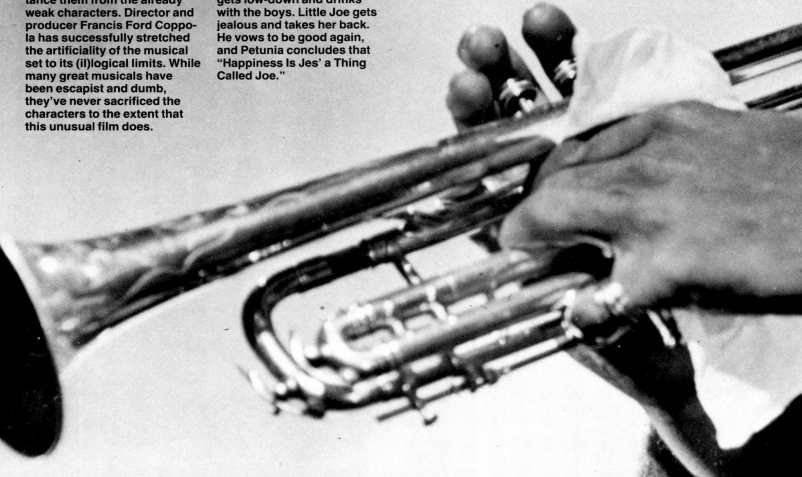

Louis Armstrong was a natural choice for Gabriel in the supernatural section of Cabin in the Sky.

In the difficult transition from silent to sound filmmaking, studios were willing to experiment with any sort of musical. Because the form of the musical was not very clearly defined, some very strange hybrids slipped through the cracks.

The oddest of all was Cecil B. DeMille's **MADAM SATAN** (1930). DeMille was known for mixing sex and spectacle. Later he would hide his preoccupations in such Biblical epics as *The Ten Commandments,* but *Madam Satan* applies his style to musicals, with strange results.

In a fair imitation of Lubitsch's sex farces, the film deals with marital infidelity among the upper class. It gets rolling in the second half at a costume party held aboard a dirigible. Many guests come in semi-nude outfits. One woman is dressed as Innocent Pride because (as she explains) she has nothing to hide. Another is dressed as the Call of the Wild, wearing a lion pelt over one breast. Once on the airship, a musical number takes place. The theme of the party is The Modern Age. The dance number consists mainly of people showing off their costumes and disappearing. DeMille superimposes moving gears over the dancers in order to represent a giant carburetor, which in turn is supposed to represent the modern era (which does not explain why some of the men are dressed in Roman costumes and only partially explains why one is dressed as the God of Electricity). The net effect is an art deco version of Dante's *Inferno.* All in all it's quite strange, and not a little camp.

Fred Astaire had one of the most consistent screen personas of any actor. He lit cigarettes with class, dressed with class, and danced with class. **FOLLOW THE FLEET** (1936) is unusual because it tampers with that image.

Astaire is remarkably unconvincing as a sailor. Representative of the problem is the fact that Astaire's best friend in the film is named Bilge (Randolph Scott). This refined man couldn't really know anyone named Bilge. In an attempt to show that he is unrefined, Astaire chews gum constantly, but the effect is laughable.

Still, *Follow the Fleet* has some of the most brilliant dances ever put on the screen, due to the superb score by Irving Berlin and the presence of Ginger Rogers, Astaire's best dancing partner. The film opens with Fred Astaire dancing on deck with a jazz band accompaniment, singing "We joined the Navy to see the world, but what did we see? We saw the sea." The next number is irresistible: Rogers clad in a tight sailor outfit sings the pulsating, "Let Yourself Go"; then Astaire and Rogers do just that in one of their most energetic dances.

Follow the Fleet also contains one of Astaire and Rogers' best comic dances, "I'm Putting All My Eggs in One Basket." Through careful timing they knock about, kick each other, and once Astaire even lets Rogers drop to the floor with a smash. It is well in keeping with the foolish tone of the film.

IT'S ALWAYS FAIR WEATHER (1955) stars Gene Kelly in a semi-savage attack on the broken dreams of the 1950s. Kelly's happy-go-lucky demeanor is subdued beneath a quagmire of real problems that musicals rarely admit exist. Though the MGM ethic caused the film to back down with an unwarranted happy ending, it still leaves one feeling disoriented.

Three WW II buddies who part after the war vow to meet each other in ten years. What they're up to in 1955 is no good. Gene

Kelly is a professional gambler and bum, Dan Dailey is an advertising executive with an ulcer, and Michael Kidd is a boring hick with a wife and eight children. These old friends find that they hate each other, though by the end they have become friends again.

It's Always Fair Weather has several outstanding musical numbers. When the three buddies go on a drunken rampage through New York—dancing on a taxi, climbing around the street, and finally ending up in a dark alley—they each put their foot through a garbage can lid and do a loud shuffle which somehow manages to simultaneously be awkward and graceful.

It's Always Fair Weather.

The God of Electricity managed to show up for the costume ball in *Madam Satan*. *He must have been in a bad mood for a bolt of lightning destroys the dirigible in which the party is being held.*

133

Lampoons of horror films and sex are rare, so **THE ROCKY HORROR PICTURE SHOW** (1975) is an unusual musical based on that alone. There is more to the story, however, because this film represents the first time that the movie audience has eclipsed the movie itself.

A *Rocky Horror* cult surrounds the film and packs theatres for weekly nationwide midnight showings. Many parts of the film are clever twists on old horror films—like having the mad Dr. Frank N Furter (Tim Curry) create not a monster, but a real hunk of a man with whom the doctor (being a "cute transvestite from trans-sexual Transylvania") falls in love. After a while, these parodies appeal only to the dedicated horror movie buff. For others, the film gets garbled towards the end as the in-jokes increase and wit decreases. The cult, however, changes things.

The high points of the film often occur off-screen. Cultists dance and sing along with the film, dressing up as major characters. Cultists also interact with the film in other ways. In the early wedding sequence, when Brad proposes to Janet, fans throw rice at the screen and the other theatre patrons. When their cars get stuck in the rain in front of the mysterious castle, the addicts shoot water pistols into the air. Audience participation varies from theatre to theatre, but to assure a certain standardization there are newsletters keeping people abreast of what is in and what is out.

Because the audience is so active, it doesn't matter whether the film is any good. As it happens, the film by itself is fairly good. The fans have made *Rocky Horror* into an even more interesting film. Since the audience is the key and the film is not, *The Rocky Horror Picture Show* remains the only film whose quality varies from week to week and from city to city.

PHANTOM OF THE PARADISE (1974) is an unoriginal but amusing slapdash horror musical. It was directed by Brian De Palma, who would later direct *The Fury* and *Carrie*. Fortunately, it is his only musical.

Mixing *The Phantom of the Opera* with *Faust* in a tale about an evil record producer who steals music, the film is often a lot of fun. Frequent self-kidding—over-dramatic cello music on the soundtrack, inter-titles (such as "Later that night . . .") and deliberately over-written dialogue (like "the karma around here is so thick you need an aqualung to breathe")—lets the audience in on the joke that this is a cartoon.

The cast is very good. Paul Williams is maliciously evil and sleazy as the devil's surrogate. William Finley plays a marvelously naive optimist who wigs out at the end. Gerrit Graham is very funny as the effeminate singer, and Jessica Harper sings well but doesn't have much else to do.

The core of the film are the musical parodies by Paul Williams. He does a good job writing parodies of 1950s rock 'n' roll and Beach Boys tunes, though his modern music is not as good.

The Phantom of the Paradise is at times an amiably stupid film. With some original touches and a better script it might have worked, but originality has never come easily to De Palma. Perhaps it's a coincidence that this film is about someone who cannot create and can only take. Perhaps not.

Dr. Frank N Furter (Tim Curry) does his floor show act in front of the RKO motion picture studio logo in The Rocky Horror Picture Show. *He ends the act with a water ballet in a pool decorated with the creation scene from Michelangelo's Sistine Chapel painting.*

In Phantom of the Paradise, *William Finley must hide his face behind a mask after it is crushed in a record-molding machine.*

CAN HEIRONYMUS MERKIN EVER FORGET MERCY HUMPPE AND FIND TRUE HAPPINESS? (1969) is the first and probably only film of its kind: a surreal, egotistic, x-rated musical. As sex films go, it is soft, but bizarre enough to be worth seeing.

The film follows Heironymus Merkin (Anthony Newley) as he goes through a variety of women. He falls in lust with Mercy Humppe after making love to her on a carousel. But Mercy Humppe disappears, so Merkin goes after another woman named Polyester Poontang (Joan Collins), whom he gets pregnant and must marry. To add a touch of religious symbolism, Heironymus climbs a mountain to talk to God. Nothing happens, because God is out. Next, the girl of his dreams, Trampolena Whambang, is created (baked in a pizza oven) and they make love. Eventually the film ends.

Unbelievably this is a musical with over 13 songs. Each one has an attitude problem. "Oh What a Son of a Bitch I Am," in which Newley praises himself for all the virgins he's deflowered, is egotistic; "Once Upon a Time," a fairy tale in which a princess marries a donkey, is smugly whimsical. Of the actual clumsy execution of these songs, the less said the better.

With **THE BOY FRIEND** (1971), director Ken Russell took the happy-go-lucky musicals of the 1920s and turned them into a vehicle for despair. He went to great and complicated pains to achieve this dubious goal.

Russell does everything possible to de-glamorize the musical. The movie is set in the 1920s at an afternoon performance of *The Boy Friend.* The framed musical is not performed by eager young actors, but by bored, horrible people, only in

it for the meager money. All of the shabbiness is lovingly shown. Frequent shots of the scattered audience and long shots of the stage highlight the cheap sets, harsh lighting and bad make-up.

In the small audience is a famous movie director, Max de Thrill. His function is to inject real musical numbers into this film by imagining what might have been. Some of his dances are spectacular. For example, he envisions a huge phonograph danced on by a large chorus, which magically splits in two à la Busby Berkeley. These "imaginary" dances are the high point of the film.

The plot is a cynical rebuke to *42nd Street.* Understudy Twiggy replaces the star and doesn't know the songs or the dances. No one cares if she's any good because it's an empty house. The point—that musicals are usually unrealistic

—is well taken, but if the world is as dreary as *The Boyfriend* paints it, there *is* a real need for escapist musicals.

Mr. Scorpio does his bit for "The Astrological Ballet" from Can Heironymus Merkin Ever Forget Mercy Humppe and Find True Happiness?

PENNIES FROM HEAVEN

(1981) is a modern musical that tries to come to grips with the effect old musicals had on people. It contrasts the story of a restless, frustrated sheet-music salesman during the Depression with the light musical numbers of that era. The concept works because the dances are so good.

All of the musical numbers are wonderful and, as the film becomes more and more depressing, they become more and more elaborate (climaxing in a scene in which Steve Martin watches Fred Astaire dance to "Let's Face the Music and Dance" and then enters the screen doing his own Astaire dance). In one sequence, Martin buys lunch for a bum. They sit in a dingy luncheonette. Suddenly the bum looks at Martin and sings "Pennies from Heaven," actually mouthing an old recording. The camera pulls back and the walls of the diner separate, leaving Martin's table next to a rainstorm: the bum steps outside dancing in the rain to a relaxed violin solo, then pennies tumble from all sides in slow motion. It is a beautiful dance, but the context emphasizes how false the song's message is: it did not rain pennies for out-of-work people during the Depression. Martin has been sold a false bill of goods; he actually believes the words of the songs he sells.

Bernadette Peters, as the school teacher with whom Martin has an affair, has a flashy musical number. Her fantasies seem to come true, as she mouths the song "Love is Good for Anything That Ails You," wearing a slinky, low-cut white dress, accompanied by children on tiny white pianos and other white instruments. Peters believes the song's premise, and as a result gets pregnant and loses her job.

The film is flawed by an overly melodramatic script. It should be enough that Martin's life is miserable because he is broke, frustrated, and doesn't love his wife, but at the end he is also falsely accused of murder! The film hammers the message home a little too hard.

Steve Martin tries hard to be a hoofer in Pennies From Heaven, *but has too many great previous performances to compete with.*

Bette Midler was certainly not lacking any experience in portraying a singer in concert. She was able to draw on her own considerable singing style while maintaining "The Rose's" Janis Joplin-like character.

Can a musical be a documentary? The following films are so realistic, so honest about the private lives of performers, so unromantic, that they take on a documentary quality. It is significant that these are recent films—their personality oriented styles seem derived from the approach of television.

In **THE ROSE** (1979) show business is portrayed as both a salvation and as a trap—salvation, because it affords Mary Rose Foster "The Rose" a chance to escape her small town upbringing and enter the fast-paced world of rock 'n' roll; a trap, because the rock world is draining and the pressure of constant performance destroys her. This conflict is brilliantly brought to the screen by Bette Midler, a superstar in her own right.

The world of rock 'n' roll, as shown in the film, is brutal. There is nonstop travel, pressure, and performance. First and foremost, rock 'n' roll is a business, and the stars are just a commodity. For instance, when The Rose announces she's going to take a break from performing, her manager (Alan Bates) forbids it. Then he gives her some drugs to help her feel better. They are friends, but he also sees her as an investment that must pay off.

The Rose would not work without Bette Midler. She has a complex personality: vulnerable (crying when an old-time country and western singer says he doesn't like the way she recorded his songs), impulsive (starting a fight in a restaurant where they "don't serve hippies"), and self-

mocking (joining a nightclub's female impersonator in his version of "The Rose"). The concert footage is dynamic because Midler brings this mix of emotions to every song.

LADY SINGS THE BLUES (1972) presents the tragic story of Billie Holliday, one of the world's greatest singers. There is enough material in Holliday's life for several movies.

Diana Ross is very good as Billie Holliday. As a child, she is a timid, vulnerable girl, made even more so by being raped. After Holliday becomes a star—the first black performer to get a booking at Carnegie Hall—she is still haunted by her past. Ross's performance overcomes the sometimes sketchy script, making the character almost understandable.

Though Ross is an excellent actress, the true mark of her success in this film is her singing. She evokes Holliday's style without imitating her, and captures the screen with every song. Most of the songs are done in a nightclub setting. But in one powerful moment, Holliday's bus passes the aftermath of a lynching; as she sees the black men hanging from the trees, "Strange Fruit" comes on the soundtrack, with a haunting effect.

COAL MINER'S DAUGHTER (1980) tells the story of country and western singer Loretta Lynn and how she made it to the top. In this film, as in many movie biographies, there is a sharp dividing line between the section where the star becomes a star and the section where the star is a star. Ironically, Lynn seems more interesting as an ordinary woman than as a celebrity.

The story of her early years is fascinating and gripping. Lynn was a coal miner's daughter who married at 14 and had several children. Life seemed bleak until her husband discovered her singing ability. Then, through an amazing promotional tour—driving across the country and meeting radio managers—her husband turned Loretta into a star.

Perhaps the most extraordinary thing about *Coal Miner's Daughter* is Sissy Spacek's spectacular performance. Spacek is perhaps the only actress alive who can convincingly play a 14-year-old and a 30-year-old in the same film.

NASHVILLE (1975) is Robert Altman's poetic statement about America. The film doesn't so much tell a story as present a collage of impressions about one week in the lives of 24 people. *Nashville* is a stunning and important work that expands the idea of what a film can be.

Nashville is the capital of country music—mecca of dreams and aspirations. Each of the characters responds to the dream differently, but it is clear that Altman is examining what it is that each person wants out of life. At the end the characters converge at a political rally where the cost of those dreams is examined.

The characters are remarkable. There are country music stars out to perpetuate their fame (Henry Gibson and Karen Black) and struggling to hang on to sanity (Ronee Blakely); there are rock stars (Keith Carradine) and groupies (Shelley Duvall) on the make. There are aspiring country singers (Barbara Harris and Gwen Welles), a fruity reporter from the BBC (Geraldine Chaplin), a gospel singer and housewife (Lily Tomlin), a political organizer (Michael Murphy), and a lawyer (Ned Beatty). In short, there are people seeking the American dream in every way they can.

The complex interweaving of characters provides the loose framework for the film, and the music provides the continuity. There is lots of country music in this film, most of it written by the actors and actresses who sing it. The ironies pile up, but the film is not a satire. It simply looks at the absurdity and sincerity of its characters' lives and lets it flow.

THE WORST MUSICALS

CHAINED FOR LIFE (1951)
LOST HORIZON (1973)
YES, GIORGIO (1982)
ANNIE (1982)
LISZTOMANIA (1975)
PAJAMA PARTY (1964)
SGT. PEPPER'S LONELY
  HEARTS CLUB BAND (1978)
AT LONG LAST LOVE (1975)
MAN OF LA MANCHA (1972)
XANADU (1980)

*"I'm a worthless check, a total wreck, a flop.
But if baby, I'm the bottom, you're the top."*

*"You're the Top"
Cole Porter*

*Roger Daltry fails to out-act the scenery in Ken Russell's
Lisztomania.*

141

Have you ever been troubled by the question of Siamese Twins? Do they lead normal lives? Do they dream about being separated? Do they ever fall in love? Can they act? CHAINED FOR LIFE (1951) insists on answering these questions, whether you're prepared for the answers or not.

Chained for Life is a bad and cheaply made movie about Siamese twins. It stars the Hilton sisters (Daisy and Violet), genuine Siamese twins who made their screen debut in the classic horror film Freaks. After that there was a lull in their career; there were few films which could showcase their talents (being attached to each other at the waist and sharing several organs). But in 1951 Ross Frisco came up with a story idea that seemed a natural for the Hilton sisters.

In Chained for Life, the Hilton sisters play the featured attraction in a sleazy vaudeville house. Also on the bill is a man who plays the accordian while riding around on a bicycle and a Rumanian knife-throwing and trick sharpshooting act.

Daisy Hilton falls in love with the knife-thrower (greasily overacted by Mario Laval), perhaps because she symbolically wants him to cut her free from her sister. Violet knows that he is a bad character, but Daisy is blind to reason. Her sole concern is working out the logistics of her wedding night.

Daisy dreams that she is separated from her sister (thanks to cleverly placed bushes and trees). Totally free, she dances joyously with her man. The scene is both eerie and pathetic.

Mario plans to desert Daisy as soon as he gets her money. Violet finds out about this (so does Daisy—it's hard to avoid), and during a performance she picks up a gun and kills him. The twins are taken to jail, and the film ends with their trial. The judge realizes that he can't condemn one without condemning the other. He turns to the audience and pleads for sympathy: "What would you do?" he asks, and the film ends.

Few people have ever heard of Chained for Life because it is an exploitation film that did not play in legitimate theatres. It is so badly put together that all of the elements of a film that are normally taken for granted fall apart. For example, in every scene in the vaudeville house, no matter how many weeks apart in story time, the audience is the same; it's not meant to be the same, but one piece of stock film is used over and over again. Chained for Life is a terrible movie, but it's compelling. Even though it capitalizes on the suffering of others, one watches it to see how low it will sink.

142

The Hilton sisters (Daisy and Violet) never really adjusted to their career as glamorous Hollywood Siamese twins. They ended their days as check-out girls in a supermarket (with special cash register aisles to accommodate them).

LOST HORIZON (1973) epitomizes the bad musical. Some flawed musicals have their occasional good moments, catchy songs, or good performances, but *Lost Horizon* successfully avoids all of these possibilities.

The story is about a group of strangers on an airplane that gets hijacked and flown to a point unknown. The passengers include Sally Kellerman, a fidgeting, neurotic writer; Bobby Van, a comedian; Peter Finch, who just looks worried; and Michael York, playing Finch's brother. Then there is the mysterious George Kennedy, who introduces himself as "somebody flying in a strange plane to a strange place with a lunatic pilot and I'm trying to find out why, that's who I am." With that everyone lapses into silence.

The plane crashes somewhere in the Himalayan mountains, and a nomadic tribe rescues the passengers. They are confused because the first Oriental they meet is Sir John Gielgud talking in fortune-cookie English. They are led to Shangri-La, a utopian society in which no one ages.

Along the way the characters sing (or try to sing) some of the worst songs ever written by Burt Bacharach and Hal David. Every time the film comes close to creating a mystical mood, the songs wipe out the effect. For instance, the opening shots of clouds and mountains are almost beautiful. Then a guitar chord sounds and a singer croons, "Have you ever dreamed of a place far away from it all?" Most repulsive is the ancient Shangri-La ritual celebrating birth and the family, which sounds like the music dentists use to welcome their patients. Hal David does not understand that lyrics are supposed to do more than rhyme. The height of stupidity is reached when Bobby Van, trying to teach a classroom of kids, sings "Question Me an Answer," which is as incoherent as it sounds.

The passengers of the crashed airplane can't believe their eyes as they enter Shangri-La. Their contracts didn't prepare them for a movie this bad.

144

The characters also try to dance in some of the clumsiest numbers ever filmed. They are the work of Hermes Pan, who formerly choreographed dances for Fred Astaire; anyone can have a bad day. In "The World is a Circle," Liv Ullmann walks up a garden path followed by a line of untalented kids trying desperately to swing their arms back and forth in time to the music. In perhaps the most well-known song from the film, "Living Together," men dressed in red uniforms trudge through the town with the weary look of foot-soldiers who've been in battle too long.

While Shangri-La was dedicated to preserving the greatest achievements of mankind, there was another land nearby which preserved mankind's lowest achievements. Every so often, they screen *Lost Horizon*.

Inflated egos have resulted in many of the finest bad musicals; **YES, GIORGIO** (1982) (centered around one of the greatest egos of them all— operatic tenor Luciano Pavarotti) is awful in a grandiose way. This vain film assumes that its main character can do anything. Pavarotti plays Gior-

Annie *(Aileen Quinn)*.

Yes, Giorgio *(Luciano Pavarotti and Kathryn Harold)*.

gio Fini, who is modestly described as the world's greatest tenor. Wherever Pavarotti goes he is surrounded by groups of fawning people who love him and will do anything for him. An entire restaurant closes down just to serve Pavarotti and his date, Kathryn Harold, for free.

As bad films go, *Yes, Giorgio* contains an embarrassment of riches, especially Pavarotti's dialogue. When Kathryn Harold, a throat specialist, first meets him, he says, in his barely articulate fashion, that she is "No doctor. Is a nurse!"

When they go out, he modestly says, "You must promise you will not fall in love with me, I know it will be hard." Later when she says that opera puts her to sleep, he responds "That is because you have never heard me sing."

ANNIE (1982) is, unfortunately, quite exceptional. It is a $40-million movie that wouldn't be worth mentioning, except that it squandered so much talent and money with such poor results that it joins the ranks of great musical disasters. The only thing the movie had going for it was hype.

Annie was adapted from the long-running Broadway musical, which was based on the long-running comic strip "Little Orphan Annie." "Little Orphan Annie" told the adventures of a spunky girl who survived the Depression by using the philosophy that anyone can succeed if they have drive. In *Annie*-the-movie, as in the stage show, that concept is completely twisted. The revised philosophy shows that it is the government's role to take care of people (so Franklin Roosevelt and the New Deal are brought in), and if the government can't do it there is always a rich benefactor like Daddy Warbucks to fix everything.

The plot, very simply, is about cute orphans. The orphanage is run by the drunken, neurotic, Mrs. Hannigan (Carol Burnett), who refers to her wards as "little pig droppings." Her problem is that she can't keep the orphans from breaking out into joyous song-and-dance routines at the slightest provocation. The orphan who sings the loudest is Annie (Aileen Quinn), so Hannigan hates her the most. When Grace Farrell (Ann Reinking), secretary to billionaire Oliver Warbucks (Albert Finney), comes to borrow an orphan to live with Warbucks for the week, Hannigan tries to hide Annie, but to no avail. Annie is chosen and meets Warbucks, who is first cold and businesslike, and then succumbs to her charm.

An extraordinary thing about *Annie* is that it was directed by John Huston. Huston is known for such gloomy films as *The Maltese Falcon*—certainly not the ideal director for a film about dogs and children. Huston cannot be blamed for the uniformly bad dance numbers, however, because they were directed by Joe Layton. The choreography consists mainly of people doing cartwheels and jumping around aimlessly. Many of the numbers, like "It's the Hard Knocks Life" (which follows the orphans throughout the whole orphanage as they clean), are completely in-

coherent. The only number which works is "Easy Street," in which Mrs. Hannigan, her brother (Tim Curry), and his girlfriend (Bernadette Peters) dance through the orphanage. It is a beautifully timed comedy number, with Mrs. Hannigan constantly taking a wrong step and walking into a doorframe or kicking a hole in a wall. It is slight, but compared to everything else in the film it stands out like a gem.

The acting veers between overactors and underactors. Of the overactors, Quinn and Reinking are the hardest to take; both are perpetually on the verge of bubbling over. Burnett's performance is a much needed antidote to the cuteness, although she overplays her role, too. In the underactors' camp, Albert Finney gets to act stern (which he does well), and Geoffrey Holder (Punjab) waves his hands nicely.

One can always look to Ken Russell for the bad movie, but in **LISZTOMANIA** (1975) he got carried away with himself, and the results are horrible.

Ken Russell explores the grotesque sexual fantasy in Lisztomania.

The film treats Franz Liszt as the Mick Jagger of his day. While Liszt did attract huge crowds for his virtuoso performances, he did not have groupies who fainted while he played (as he does in the film). The updated biography concept is quickly tossed aside in favor of cheap shots. Richard Wagner shows up as a little child in a sailor suit, with a cap

that says S.S. Nietzsche. This subtle political analogy is followed by Wagner marrying Liszt's daughter and appearing as Count Dracula. Later Liszt finds Wagner in an Austrian village where the villagers (Jewish pawnbrokers) act as though he were Dr. Frankenstein. It turns out that he is like Frankenstein, creating not a monster but a perfect Aryan. After Wagner is killed, Hitler rises from his grave carrying a machine gun shaped like a guitar and guns down Jews while a chorus of blond-haired boys in Superman costumes dance in the background.

A film like *Lisztomania* can make one angry. There is certainly enough imagination in the film for several movies, but it is squandered and self-indulgently tossed away.

No list of worst musicals would be complete without a Beach Party Movie. This strange breed of films came into being in the mid-1960s, made big money for sharp promotors like Samuel Z. Arkoff, and then went to a well-deserved demise. In the 1960s, youth rebelled against parents, took over colleges, and mounted protests. The makers of Beach Party Movies seemed to have an inkling that teenagers were doing something different, but they weren't sure what.

Films like **PAJAMA PARTY** (1964) make it clear that the youth of America are interested only in playing volleyball, swimming, dancing and making out on the beach (to the sounds of Beach Boys-style music). *Pajama Party* has every possible thing wrong with it. It is a comedy, yet the only jokes are sight gags the Three Stooges would have been ashamed to use. They are so feeble that every joke is accompanied with a "Boiiiing" or a "Wuah, wuah, wuah" on the soundtrack.

The stupid story features Annette Funicello as the girl with the biggest breasts; Elsa Lanchester as an eccentric woman who likes the free-wheeling teens so much that

she sells them really cool clothing at well below wholesale; and Jesse "Mr. Maytag" White as a professional burglar with a blond Swedish assistant and an Indian companion (Buster Keaton). Jesse White wants to burgle the rich eccentric's house, and a Martian (Tommy Kirk) is supposed to overrun the earth, but instead falls in love with Annette.

Sgt. Pepper's Lonely Hearts Club Band.

Some movies are doomed from the start by moronic concepts. **SGT. PEPPER'S LONELY HEARTS CLUB BAND** (1978) is an opera built around Beatles' songs that stars the Bee Gees and Alice Cooper. Director Robert Stigwood wasted millions of dollars financing it.

The first problem with this fiasco was self-imposed: the characters never speak and only sing Beatles' songs. This created a bind, leaving no logical way for the story to be explained (which really worked out fine since there was no logical story either). George Burns fills the gap by narrating the film. The story, as far as can be determined, involves the conflict between the forces of good and evil. The Bee Gees (as the forces of good) try to find Sgt. Pepper's original instruments, and the forces of evil try to stop them.

Because all the Beatles' songs already have definitive interpretations as recorded by the Beatles, the many Bee Gees renditions simply aren't good enough. And all are badly staged and badly filmed. All of this might have been excused if the songs made any sense in the context of the film, but none of them do.

Annette Funicello made a beach party career out of hanging ten in her transition from Mouseketeer to peanut butter spokesperson.

Eileen Brennan, Cybill Shepherd, and Madeline Kahn do the elephant stomp to Cole Porter's elegant tunes in At Long Last Love.

In *Singin' in the Rain* it is said of the Lina Lamont character that "She can't sing, she can't dance, she can't act. A triple threat!" Those lines perfectly describe Cybill Shepherd, who with some help turned **AT LONG LAST LOVE** (1975) into the disaster it is.

Shepherd's appearance in the film can be blamed on director/writer/producer Peter Bogdanovich. Bogdanovich had already succeeded in reviving the old movie genres in such films as *What's Up Doc?* A musical was the logical next step. Bogdanovich didn't want to make just any musical though; he wanted to make a screwball comedy musical starring Shepherd (with whom he was then living). To fill out the bill, Bogdanovich got Burt Reynolds, a man who had never performed light comedy and could not sing, and Madeline Kahn, who was mis-cast because she *could* sing, act, and dance.

The film they stomped their way through is painful to talk about. There is a vague plot involving romantic mis-alliances. There are vague dance numbers choreographed to resemble kids killing worms with their feet. There is "clever dialogue," such as Reynolds complaining incessantly that he's bored by the fact that it's six o'clock: "I'm sick of six," he says.

Shepherd, however, carries the film away. As an actress she has mastered the pout and little else, but she has such a variety of pouts who could complain? There is her "I'm angry" pout, her "I'm in love" pout, and an "I'm concentrating on trying to sing" pout. One of the songs in *At Long Last Love* is Cole Porter's "You're the Top," and as far as bad musicals go *At Long Last Love* is certainly up there.

The most obvious problem with **MAN OF LA MANCHA** (1972), a film about the mad-man Don Quixote who thinks he is a knight, is the casting. Peter O'Toole as Quixote bellows and overacts. Still, he might have been tolerable in the role if he had the slightest singing ability—but he doesn't. In the good old days, actors who couldn't sing were dubbed. Today, that is considered dishonest, so O'Toole's version of "The Impossible Dream" can bring tears to one's eyes.

Peter O'Toole and James Coco in Man of La Mancha.

Director Arthur Hiller proved that he had not the slightest conception of what a musical is, and even less understanding of *Man of La Mancha.* On Broadway, the show worked because there was an air of fantasy about it—when Quixote battles windmills, thinking they were dragons, only the aftermath was shown. Thus the audience could see that Quixote was crazy, and yet not see his humiliation. We respected his madness. In the film, the windmill fight is clumsily and painfully shown, making Quixote seem not crazy, but stupid. Instead of being filmed in a gentle fantasy style, the movie is directed as if it were a documentary on fishing.

The movie has some curio value (because one has few opportunities to hear Sophia Loren try to sing), but little else. Instead of being the picture it could have been, *Man of La Mancha* became the possible nightmare.

151

XANADU (1980) is the ultimate disco movie—all flashy images, high tech effects, and nothing else.

It is easy to see where the movie went wrong—it features Olivia Newton-John on roller skates as a muse sent from heaven to Earth to inspire artists.

Certainly no one inspired the choreographer of this film. The legendary Gene Kelly makes one appearance in which he absolutely outclasses the film. It is a waste of his tremendous talent. The stupidity of the other numbers is best illustrated by the nightclub scene, which starts out in an abandoned warehouse which is going to be used for the nightclub. "What shall I call the place?" asks the dim-witted hero of the film. Newton-John appears and recites "In Xanadu did Kubla Khan…." "Great," the dim-witted hero says, "We'll call it Khan's…." Next, Gene Kelly and the kid each imagine what "Xanadu" will look like. Kelly envisions a 1940s nightclub with a swing band. The kid imagines a roller-skating disco. Suddenly the two images merge, creating a roller-skating disco with jazzy overtones. A mob of people jump and spin. The entertainment value is akin to watching war newsreels while someone shines a bright light in your eye.

Not all popular performers are meant for the cinema. Not even Olivia Newton-John's vocal powers could add anything cinematically to Xanadu. While the ineptitude of the film-makers made everyone look bad, Newton-John proved to have a singular lack of screen charisma when she was teamed up with one who has plenty to spare: Gene Kelly (right). She was able to turn the songs from the film into radio hits, though. Her voice seems to imply more than her image promises.

RATING GUIDE

FILM	YEAR	RATING	DIRECTOR	STAR	CATEGORY	TIME	DISTRIBUTOR
All That Jazz	1979	7	Bob Fosse	Roy Scheider	Show Biz Folks	119	CBS
An American in Paris	1951	8	Vincente Minnelli	Gene Kelly	Faraway Places	113	MGM
Anchors Aweigh	1945	7	George Sidney	Gene Kelly	Fairy Tales	103	N/A
Annie	1982	2	John Huston	Aileen Quinn	Worst	115	CHV
At Long Last Love	1975	1	Peter Bogdanovich	Cybil Shepherd	Worst	115	N/A
Babes in Arms	1939	8	Busby Berkeley	Garland/Rooney	Backstage	97	N/A
Band Wagon, The	1953	9	Vincente Minnelli	Fred Astaire	Backstage	112	MGM
Barkleys of Broadway, The	1948	7	Charles Walters	Astaire/Rogers	Show Biz Folks	110	N/A
Belle of New York, The	1952	7	Charles Walters	Fred Astaire	Show Biz Folks	82	N/A
Bells Are Ringing	1960	8	Vincente Minnelli	Judy Holiday	Americana	126	MGM
Best Little Whorehouse in Texas, The	1982	5	Colin Higgins	Dolly Parton	Americana	N/A	N/A
Big Broadcast of 1938	1938	7	Mitchell Leisen	Bob Hope	Show Biz Folks	9	N/A
Blue Hawaii	1962	5	Norman Taurog	Elvis Presley	Rock 'n' Roll	101	CBS
Blue Skies	1946	7	Stuart Heisler	Astaire/Crosby	Show Biz Folks	104	N/A
Blues Brothers, The	1980	6	John Landis	John Belushi	Show Biz Folks	130	MCA
Boy Friend, The	1972	6	Ken Russell	Twiggy	Most Unusual	N/A	N/A
Breaking Glass	1980	6	Brian Gibson	Hazel O'Connor	Rock 'n' Roll	104	PHV
Brigadoon	1954	8	Vincente Minnelli	Gene Kelly	Fairy Tales	108	MGM
Broadway Melody	1929	7	Harry Beaumont	Bessie Love	Backstage	110	N/A
Broadway Melody of 1940	1940	7	Norman Taurog	Fred Astaire	Show Biz Folks	102	N/A
Buddy Holly Story, The	1978	9	Steve Rash	Gary Busey	Rock 'n' Roll	114	N/A
Bugsy Malone	1976	7	Alan Parker	Jodie Foster	Americana	93	PHV
Bye Bye Birdie	1963	9	George Sidney	Ann-Margret	Americana	111	CHV
Cabaret	1972	9	Bob Fosse	Liza Minnelli	Backstage	119	CBS
Cabin in the Sky	1943	7	Vincente Minnelli	Lena Horne	Most Unusual	100	N/A
Camelot	1967	7	Josh Logan	Richard Harris	Fairy Tales	150	WHV
Can Can	1960	5	Walter Lang	Shirley MacLaine	Faraway Places	131	N/A
Can't Stop the Music	1980	3	Nancy Walker	Village People	Rock 'n' Roll	120	TH
Can Heironymus Merkin....	1969	6	Anthony Newley	Milton Berle	Most Unusual	106	N/A
Carefree	1938	7	Mark Sandrich	Astaire/Rogers	Show Biz Folks	83	NM
Carmen Jones	1955	7	Otto Preminger	Harry Belafonte	Americana	105	N/A
Carousel	1956	7	Henry King	Gordon MacRae	Fairy Tales	128	N/A
Chained for Life	1951	0	Henry L. Fraser	Hilton Sisters	Worst	75	N/A
Chitty Chitty Bang Bang	1968	4	Ken Hughes	Dick Van Dyke	Fairy Tales	142	CBS
Coal Miner's Daughter	1980	8	Michael Apted	Sissy Spacek	Most Unusual	125	MCA
Curly Top	1935	7	Irving Cummings	Shirley Temple	Fairy Tales	N/A	N/A
Damsel in Distress	1937	7	George Stevens	Fred Astaire	Fairy Tales	101	N/A
Divine Madness	1980	8	Michael Ritchie	Bette Midler	Rock 'n' Roll	94	WHV
Dr. Doolittle	1967	6	Richard Fleisher	Rex Harrison	Fairy Tales	144	CBS
Easter Parade	1948	8	Charles Walters	Astaire/Garland	Americana	103	N/A
Easy Come, Easy Go	1967	5	John Rich	Elvis Presley	Rock 'n' Roll	95	PHV
Fame	1980	8	Alan Parker	Irene Cara	Backstage	133	CBS
Fiddler on the Roof	1971	6	Norman Jewison	Topol	Faraway Places	184	CBS
Five Thousand Fingers of Dr. T., The	1953	9	Roy Rowland	Hans Conreid	Fairy Tales	88	N/A
Flying Down to Rio	1933	8	Thornton Freeland	Astaire/Rogers	Faraway Places	89	NM
Follow the Fleet	1936	7	Mark Sandrich	Astaire/Rogers	Most Unusual	110	NM
Footlight Parade	1933	8	Lloyd Bacon	James Cagney	Backstage	90	N/A
For Me and My Gal	1942	7	Busby Berkeley	Judy Garland	Show Biz Folks	100	N/A
42nd Street	1933	10	Lloyd Bacon	Ruby Keeler	Backstage	89	CBS
Funny Face	1968	10	Stanley Donen	Fred Astaire	Faraway Places	155	N/A
Funny Girl	1968	8	William Wyler	Barbra Streisand	Show Biz Folks	155	CHV
Gang's All Here, The	1943	8	Busby Berkeley	Carmen Miranda	Show Biz Folks	103	N/A
Gay Divorcee, The	1934	8	Mark Sandrich	Astaire/Rogers	Show Biz Folks	108	NM
Gentlemen Prefer Blondes	1953	7	Howard Hawks	Marilyn Monroe	Americana	91	CBS
G.I. Blues	1960	5	Norman Taurog	Elvis Presley	Rock 'n' Roll	104	CBS
Gigi	1958	9	Vincente Minnelli	Leslie Caron	Faraway Places	119	MGM
Girl Can't Help It, The	1956	7	Frank Tashlin	Jayne Mansfield	Rock 'n' Roll	99	N/A
Girl Crazy	1943	8	Norman Taurog	Garland/Rooney	Rock 'n' Roll	105	N/A
Girls! Girls! Girls!	1962	5	Norman Taurog	Elvis Presley	Rock 'n' Roll	105	CBS
Going My Way	1944	8	Leo McCarey	Bing Crosby	Americana	126	MCA
Gold Diggers of 1933	1933	8	Mervyn LeRoy	Ruby Keeler	Backstage	96	N/A
Gold Diggers of 1935	1935	8	Busby Berkeley	Dick Powell	Backstage	90	N/A
Good News	1947	8	Charles Walters	Peter Lawford	Americana	92	N/A
Grease	1978	6	Randal Kleiser	John Travolta	Americana	110	PHV

FILM	YEAR	RATING	DIRECTOR	STAR	CATEGORY	TIME	DISTRIBUTOR
Guys and Dolls	1955	7	Joseph Mankiewicz	Marlon Brando	Americana	149	CBS
Gypsy	1962	8	Mervyn LeRoy	Natalie Wood	Show Biz Folks	194	N/A
Hair	1979	9	Milos Foreman	Treat Williams	Rock 'n' Roll	121	CBS
Hard Day's Night, A	1964	9	Richard Lester	The Beatles	Rock 'n' Roll	85	N/A
Harder They Come, The	1973	7	Perry Henzell	Jimmy Cliff	Rock 'n' Roll	93	WHV
Head	1968	7	Bob Rafelson	The Monkees	Most Unusual	86	N/A
Hello, Dolly!	1969	8	Gene Kelly	Barbra Streisand	Americana	148	CBS
Help!	1965	8	Richard Lester	The Beatles	Rock 'n' Roll	90	N/A
Holiday Inn	1942	9	Mark Sandrich	Crosby/Astaire	Backstage	101	MCA
International House	1933	8	Edward Sutherland	W. C. Fields	Faraway Places	72	N/A
It's Always Fair Weather	1955	8	Kelly/Donen	Stanley Donen	Most Unusual	101	N/A
Jailhouse Rock	1957	8	Richard Thorpe	Elvis Presley	Rock 'n' Roll	96	MGM
Jazz Singer, The	1927	7	Alan Crosland	Al Jolson	Show Biz Folks	90	CBS
Jazz Singer, The	1980	4	Richard Fleischer	Neil Diamond	Show Biz Folks	110	PHV
Jesus Christ Superstar	1973	6	Norman Jewison	Ted Neeley	Rock 'n' Roll	108	MC
King and I, The	1956	8	Walter Lang	Yul Brynner	Faraway Places	133	CBS
King Creole	1958	5	Michael Curtiz	Elvis Presley	Rock 'n' Roll	115	CBS
Kismet	1955	6	Vincente Minnelli	Howard Keel	Faraway Places	113	MGM
Kiss Me Kate	1953	7	George Sidney	Kathryn Grayson	Backstage	109	N/A
Lady Sings the Blues	1972	7	Sidney Furie	Diana Ross	Most Unusual	144	PHV
Let's Dance	1950	7	Norman Z. Leonard	Fred Astaire	Show Biz Folks	95	N/A
Lisztomania	1975	1	Ken Russell	Roger Daltrey	Worst	105	WHV
Lost Horizon	1973	0	Charles Jarrott	Sally Kellerman	Worst	134	N/A
Love Me Tonight	1932	9	Rouben Mamoulian	Maurice Chevalier	Fairy Tales	96	N/A
Love Parade, The	1929	10	Ernst Lubitsch	Maurice Chevalier	Fairy Tales	112	N/A
Loving You	1957	5	Hal Kanter	Elvis Presley	Rock 'n' Roll	101	WHV
Madam Satan	1930	7	Cecil B. DeMille	Lillian Roth	Most Unusual	105	N/A
Mame	1974	5	Gene Saks	Lucille Ball	Americana	131	N/A
Man of La Mancha	1972	2	Arthur Hiller	Peter O'Toole	Worst	140	CBS
Mary Poppins	1964	8	Robert Stevenson	Julie Andrews	Fairy Tales	140	N/A
Meet Me in St. Louis	1944	10	Vincente Minnelli	Judy Garland	Americana	113	MGM
Mother Wore Tights	1947	7	Walter Lang	Betty Grable	Americana	107	N/A
Movie, Movie	1978	7	Stanley Donen	George C. Scott	Backstage	107	N/A
Muppet Movie, The	1979	8	James Frawley	Kermit the Frog	Fairy Tales	94	CBS
Music Man, The	1962	8	Morton da Costa	Robert Preston	Americana	151	N/A
My Fair Lady	1964	8	George Cukor	Rex Harrison	Faraway Places	170	CBS
Nashville	1975	8	Robert Altman	Lily Tomlin	Most Unusual	159	PHV
New York, New York	1977	8	Martin Scorsese	Liza Minnelli	Show Biz Folks	155	CBS
Night and Day	1946	6	Michael Curtiz	Cary Grant	Show Biz Folks	128	N/A
O Lucky Man	1973	7	Lindsay Anderson	Malcolm MacDowell	Most Unusual	180	N/A
Oh! Calcutta	1972	5	N/A	Bill Macy	Most Unusual	105	VID
Oklahoma!	1955	6	Fred Zinneman	Shirley Jones	Americana	140	CBS
Oliver!	1968	8	Carol Reed	Mark Lester	Faraway Places	153	N/A
On A Clear Day You Can See Forever	1970	7	Vincente Minnelli	Barbra Streisand	Faraway Places	129	N/A
On the Town	1949	8	Kelly/Donen	Frank Sinatra	Faraway Places	98	MGM
One From the Heart	1982	8	Francis Ford Coppola	Nastassia Kinski	Most Unusual	N/A	N/A
Paint Your Wagon	1970	5	Josh Logan	Lee Marvin	Americana	164	PHV
Pajama Game, The	1958	8	Stanley Donen	Doris Day	Americana	101	N/A
Pajama Party	1964	0	Don Weis	Annette Funicello	Worst	85	N/A
Pal Joey	1957	5	George Sidney	Frank Sinatra	Americana	111	N/A
Pennies From Heaven	1981	8	Herbert Ross	Bernadette Peters	Most Unusual	107	MGM
Phantom of the Paradise	1974	6	Brian DePalma	Paul Williams	Most Unusual	92	N/A
Pink Floyd's The Wall	1982	6	Alan Parker	Bob Geldof	Rock 'n' Roll	N/A	MGM
Pinocchio	1982	6	Ben Sharpstein	Pinocchio	Fairy Tales	77	N/A
Pirate, The	1948	9	Vincente Minnelli	Judy Garland	Fairy Tales	102	MGM
Popeye	1980	8	Robert Altman	Robin Williams	Fairy Tales	114	PHV
Quadrophenia	1979	9	Marc Roddam	Phil Daniels	Rock 'n' Roll	115	N/A
Rhapsody in Blue	1945	6	Irving Rapper	Robert Alda	Show Biz Folks	93	N/A
Rhythm on the River	1940	8	Victor Schertzinger	Bing Crosby	Show Biz Folks	94	N/A
Road to Bali, The	1942	7	Hal Walker	Crosby/Hope	Faraway Places	91	UV
Roberta	1942	8	William A. Seiter	Astaire/Rogers	Show Biz Folks	85	N/A
Rocky Horror Picture Show, The	1975	8	Jim Sherman	Tim Curry	Most Unusual	100	N/A
Rock 'n' Roll High School	1979	8	Allan Arkush	P. J. Soles	Rock 'n' Roll	93	WHV
Roller Boogie	1979	3	Mark Lester	Linda Blair	Worst	103	WHV

FILM	YEAR	RATING	DIRECTOR	STAR	CATEGORY	TIME	DISTRIBUTOR
Rose Marie	1936	7	W. S. Van Dyke	Nelson Eddie	Americana	110	N/A
Rose, The	1979	8	Mark Rydell	Bette Midler	Most Unusual	134	CBS
Royal Wedding	1951	8	Stanley Donen	Fred Astaire	Faraway Places	93	MGM
Saturday Night Fever	1977	8	John Badham	John Travolta	Americana	118	MCA
Seven Brides for Seven Brothers	1954	7	Stanley Donen	Howard Keel	Americana	103	MGM
Sextette	1978	2	Ken Hughes	Mae West	Worst	91	MHE
Sgt. Peppers' Lonely Hearts Club Band	1978	2	Michael Schultz	The Bee Gees	Worst	113	MCA
Shall We Dance	1937	8	Mark Sandrich	Astaire/Rogers	Show Biz Folks	105	NM
Shock Treatment	1982	6	Jim Sharman	Richard O'Brien	Rock 'n' Roll	94	N/A
Showboat	1936	8	James Whale	Paul Robeson	Show Biz Folks	113	N/A
Showboat	1951	7	George Sidney	Kathryn Grayson	Show Biz Folks	108	MGM
Silk Stockings	1957	8	Rouben Mamoulian	Fred Astaire	Faraway Places	116	MGM
Singin' in the Rain	1952	10	Donen/Kelly	Gene Kelly	Backstage	103	MGM
Song of Norway	1970	3	Andrew Stone	Florence Henderson	Worst	139	CBS
Sound of Music, The	1965	8	Robert Wise	Julie Andrews	Faraway Places	174	CBS
South Pacific	1958	6	Josh Logan	Mitzi Gaynor	Faraway Places	167	BH
Star is Born, A	1954	8	George Cukor	Judy Garland	Show Biz Folks	150	WHV
Stormy Weather	1943	7	Andrew Stone	Lena Horne	Show Biz Folks	77	N/A
Story of Vernon and Irene Castle, The	1939	7	H. C. Potter	Astaire/Rogers	Show Biz Folks	93	NM
Summer Stock	1950	7	Charles Walters	Judy Garland	Show Biz Folks	109	N/A
Sweet Charity	1969	5	Bob Fosse	Shirley MacLaine	Fairy Tales	157	N/A
Swing Time	1936	10	George Stevens	Astaire/Rogers	Show Biz Folks	103	NM/KV
Tales of Hoffman	1951	7	Michael Powell	Moira Shearer	Fairy Tales	107	HRE
Terror of Tiny Town	1933	2	Sam Newfield	Midgets	Worst	65	BV
That's Entertainment	1974	8	Jack Haley, Jr.	Various	Survey	132	MGM
That's Entertainment Part II	1976	6	Gene Kelly	Various	Survey	133	MGM
Three Little Words	1950	8	Richard Thorpe	Fred Astaire	Show Biz Folks	102	N/A
Three Penny Opera	1932	8	G. W. Pabst	Lotte Lenya	Fairy Tales	N/A	N/A
Till the Clouds Roll By	1946	7	Richard Whorf	Judy Garland	Show Biz Folks	137	MGM
Times Square	1980	4	Alan Moyle	Trini Alvarado	Rock 'n' Roll	111	TH
Tommy	1975	6	Ken Russell	Ann-Margret	Rock 'n' Roll	110	CHV
Top Hat	1935	10	Mark Sandrich	Astaire/Rogers	Faraway Places	97	NM
Viva Las Vegas	1964	6	George Sidney	Elvis Presley	Rock 'n' Roll	86	MGM
Weekend in Havana	1941	7	Walter Long	Carmen Miranda	Show Biz Folks	80	N/A
West Side Story	1961	8	Robert Wise	Natalie Wood	Americana	151	CBS
White Christmas	1954	6	Michael Curtiz	Bing Crosby	Show Biz Folks	120	N/A
Willy Wonka and the Chocolate Factory	1971	4	Mel Stewart	Gene Wilder	Fairy Tales	98	N/A
Wiz, The	1978	7	Sidney Lumet	Diana Ross	Fairy Tales	133	MCA
Wizard of Oz, The	1939	10	Victor Fleming	Judy Garland	Fairy Tales	110	MGM
Words and Music	1948	7	Norman Taurog	Mickey Rooney	Show Biz Folks	100	N/A
Xanadu	1980	0	Robert Greenwald	Olivia Newton-John	Worst	96	MCA
Yankee Doodle Dandy	1942	8	Michael Curtiz	James Cagney	Show Biz Folks	126	MV
Yellow Submarine	1968	8	George Dunning	The Beatles	Rock 'n' Roll	85	N/A
Yes, Giorgio	1982	0	N/A	Luciano Pavarotti	Worst	N/A	MGM
Yolanda and the Thief	1945	8	Vincente Minnelli	Fred Astaire	Fairy Tales	108	N/A
Ziegfield Follies, The	1946	8	Vincente Minnelli	Fred Astaire	Fairy Tales	110	MGM

DISTRIBUTOR KEY AND ADDRESSES

BH BLACKHAWK FILMS
1235 West Fifth
Box 3990
Davenport, IA 52808
319-323-9736

BV BUDGET VIDEO
4590 Santa Monica Boulevard
Los Angeles, CA 90029
213-476-2250

CBS CBS/FOX HOME VIDEO
23705 Industrial Park Court
Farmington Hills, MI 48024
313-476-2250

CHV COLUMBIA HOME VIDEO
Columbia Plaza
Building 137
Burbank, CA 91505
213-954-3823

KV KING OF VIDEO
3529 South Valley View Boulevard
Las Vegas, NV 89103
702-362-2520
800-634-6143

MCA MCA VIDEOCASSETTE
70 Universal City Plaza
Universal City, CA 91608
213-508-4300

MHE MEDIA HOME ENTERTAINMENT
116 North Robertson Boulevard
Suite 909
Los Angeles, CA 90048
213-855-1611
800-421-4509

MGM MGM/UA HOME VIDEO
1700 Broadway
New York, NY 10019
212-975-1700

NM NOSTALGIA MERCHANT
6255 Sunset Boulevard
Suite 1019
Hollywood CA 90028
213-464-1406
800-421-4495

PHV PARAMOUNT HOME VIDEO
5555 Melrose Avenue
Los Angeles, CA 90038
213-468-5000

PLV PLANET VIDEO
1650 Broadway
Suite 1400
New York, NY 10019

SK SHEIK VIDEO CORPORATION
1823-25 Airline Highway
Metairie, LA 70001
504-833-9458
800-535-6005

TH THORN/EMI VIDEO
1370 Avenue of the Americas
New York, NY 10019
212-977-8990

TF THUNDERBIRD FILMS
3500 Verdugo Road
Box 65157
Los Angeles, CA 90065
213-256-1034

VY VIDEO YESTERYEAR
Box C
Sandy Hook, CT 06482
203-426-2574
800-243-0987

WHV WARNER HOME VIDEO INC
4000 Warner Boulevard
Burbank, CA 91522
213-954-6000

INDEX

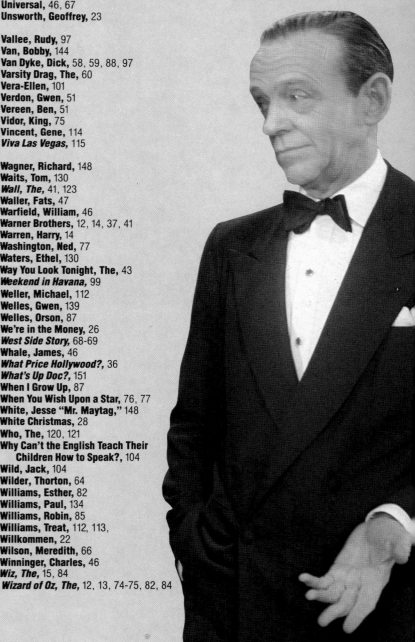